EVERY PLACE MATTERS

TOWARDS EFFECTIVE PLACE-BASED POLICY

ANDREW BEER, FIONA MCKENZIE, JIŘÍ BLAŽEK, MARKKU SOTARAUTA AND SARAH AYRES

Regional Studies Policy Impact Books
Series Editor: Philip R. Tomlinson

Regional Studies
Association

Research Today, Policy Tomorrow

First published 2020
by Taylor & Francis
4 Park Square, Milton Park, Abingdon, Oxon, OX14 4RN

Taylor & Francis Group, an informa business

© 2020 Andrew Beer, Fiona McKenzie, Jiří Blažek,
Markku Sotarauta and Sarah Ayres

British Library Cataloguing-in-Publication Data
A catalogue record for this book is available from the British Library.

Trademark notice: Product or corporate names may be trademarks or registered trademarks, and are used only for identification and explanation without intent to infringe.

ISBN13: 978-0-367-62649-5 (print)
ISBN13: 978-1-003-11011-8 (e-book)

Typeset in 10.5/13.5 Univers LT Std
by Nova Techset Private Limited, Bengaluru and Chennai, India

CONTENTS

EVERY PLACE MATTERS: TOWARDS EFFECTIVE PLACE-BASED POLICY

PREAMBLE

This publication is one of a series produced by the Regional Studies Association (RSA) in its Policy Impact book series as policy-facing documents that contribute to public debate and the development of better government programmes and policies. The series seeks to bring together cutting-edge academic knowledge with the perspectives of policy-makers at the local, national and international levels. Unlike conventional academic outputs, there is a clear focus on summarising current knowledge and experience and drawing out the implications for policy and on-the-ground efforts to advance the well-being of communities, regions and cities.

This is one of several books in the series, with earlier publications focused on: Cohesion Policy 4.0; Smart Specialisation and industry policy; and forthcoming titles which will focus on China's Belt and Road Initiative (BRI); and higher education institutions in regional development. Each book is developed by a consortium of researchers collaborating on a Policy Expo that reviews relevant academic and policy work on the topic, seeks the views of members of the RSA and reaches out to engage with policy-makers.

In this Expo we sought to develop fresh perspectives on place-based policy in three key ways:

- We ensured that we – as a research team – were at the cutting edge of knowledge through a review of recent writing on place-based policy. We went to considerable efforts to examine work from a range of informants, including: academic sources; think tanks; local, regional and national government agencies; and supra-national organisations such as the Organisation for Economic Co-operation and Development (OECD) and European Commission.

- We conducted a workshop with our colleagues attending the RSA Annual Conference in Santiago de Compostela, Spain, in June 2019, and gathered their collective insights into place-based policy. Through a semi-structured focus group discussion, we sought their perspectives on: the current state of place-based policy and its future; its interaction with place-based leadership; the factors that contribute to its success; and its role within national government programmes.

- We engineered a mediated discussion between academics and policy-makers in November 2019. As part of this exchange, we presented a summary of our findings to academics at the RSA Winter Conference and asked them to respond to our preliminary conclusions while challenging them to raise questions they would ask of policy-makers if they were present at that discussion. We also invited them to nominate the key insights or

https://doi.org/10.1080/2578711X.2020.1783890

observations they would share with senior policy-makers if they were able. The second part of this element of the project involved the conduct of a face-to-face discussion in the following week with policy-makers from the European Commission (including DG Mare, DG Regio and DG Finance). At this meeting we presented our preliminary findings as well as the questions and key lessons raised by our colleagues at the Winter Conference. In this way, the research team was able to gain an insight into both the concerns of professional researchers and the perspectives of policy-makers working at the scale of the whole of Europe.

As we completed this book, the world faced the impacts of the COVID-19 pandemic, and while the health consequences are clear and stark, the economic outcomes are equally profound and negative. Critically, at this time of challenge, governments and communities have turned to place-based solutions – the closing of borders, the restriction of local travel, a focus on community and neighbourhood – to provide support and an answer to the challenges of infection and economic disruption. The scale and impact of this pandemic emphasises that now, more than ever, robust place-based policies are needed to sustain individuals and the cities and regions in which they live.

This book is written for at least three audiences. First, it is our expectation that policy-makers will find it of value, giving them the opportunity to better understand recent trends in place-based policy and how practices can vary at the global scale. Second, we hope it will serve the needs of academics as a useful assessment of the 'state of play' of research on place-based policy. Finally, we trust it will be of benefit to regional or local development practitioners, as well as community members, in developed and developing economies alike. Amongst other things, this publication empowers communities and places to take control of their future – it gives insights into what works and does not work, and it provides examples of success and failure in seeking to deliver better economic, social and environmental outcomes locally.

In concluding, we would acknowledge that place-based policy is a global phenomenon, as international as the team that created this publication. No one nation, or group of nations (such as the European Union), has an exclusive hold on innovation or best practice in place-based policy, nor is success limited to developed nations or those with unitary or federal systems of government. This diversity of experience and perspective is not solely reflected in the geographical distribution of the research team. As authors we also have considerable experience working directly for regional government (McKenzie), providing advice to European national and regional governments (Ayres, Sotarauta and Blažek) and engaging with a federal Anglo-sphere government (Beer). As a community of policy-makers, researchers and practitioners there is an opportunity for all of us to learn from the experience of others, whether they are located three kilometres away or ten thousand.

AUTHORS

Andrew Beer is the Executive Dean, UniSA Business, University of South Australia, Adelaide. He is a Fellow of the Regional Studies Association, the Regional Australia Institute and the UK's Academy of Social Sciences. Beer has worked on regional and housing research for more than 20 years. ✉ andrew.beer@unisa.edu.au; ⓘ 0000-0002-9255-3985

Fiona McKenzie is Principal Researcher in the Victorian state government and an Adjunct Researcher at RMIT University in Melbourne, Victoria, Australia. A geographer by background, she completed her PhD by publication in the UniSA Business School in 2018. McKenzie previously worked in the Australian government's Department of Immigration and Population Research, and across several state government agencies where her work has resulted in publications on population change in rural and regional Australia. ✉ Fiona.McKenzie@delwp.vic.gov.au; ⓘ 0000-0002-9284-4184

Jiří Blažek is a Professor in the Department of Social Geography and Regional Development, Charles University, Prague. He conducts research in economic geography, in particular the formation of regional innovation systems in less developed European countries. For over 15 years he has been engaged in close cooperation with various intermediaries supporting regional development in Czechia. ✉ jiri.blazek@natur.cuni.cz; ⓘ 0000-0002-6987-3833

Markku Sotarauta is a Professor of Regional Development Studies in the Faculty of Management and Business at Tampere University, Finland. He specialises in leadership, innovation systems, and institutional entrepreneurship in city and regional development. Sotarauta has worked with the Finnish parliament, many Finnish ministries, as well as cities and regions in both Finland and other countries. ✉ Markku.Sotarauta@tuni.fi; ⓘ 0000-0001-6603-6370

Sarah Ayres is a Professor of Public Policy and Governance at the University of Bristol, UK. She is a political scientist with expertise in public administration and theories of policy-making. Her research is concerned with territorial and collaborative governance: how actors from state, market, and civil society coalesce and work with one another in specific localities. Ayres has been an academic advisor to three successive UK governments on English devolution and she regularly provides written and oral evidence to both government consultations and House of Commons inquiries. ✉ **sarah.ayres@bristol.ac.uk;** ⓘ 0000-0002-5791-6955

https://doi.org/10.1080/2578711X.2020.1783891

EXECUTIVE SUMMARY

Through this Policy Expo we have examined placed-based policy as a form of public policy, one of a potential suite of measures available to governments, and part of the apparatus and agenda-setting of the political process. Place-based policies have a focus on cities, localities or regions, but they represent far more than just a label for already established programmes of government activity, or the concentration of public sector resources in specific locations.

> *Place-based policies embody an ethos about, and an approach to, the development of economies and society that acknowledges that the context of each and every city, region and rural district offers opportunities for enhancing well-being. It advocates for a development approach tailored to the needs of each.*

Importantly, place-based policy explicitly seeks the development of all parts of the landscape, with no settlement too small or too remote to grow and develop.

We found that place-based policies can be both proactive, through a focus on innovation, and reactive, when they are used to respond to economic disruption. As policy instruments, they reflect a qualitatively different philosophy of the role of government, and the dynamics of contemporary economies, when compared with spatially blind policy settings. Place-based policies are not the exclusive domain of governments, with other actors – including universities – both contributors to, and stakeholders in, the use of such policies. Place-based policies:

- are often applied as one part of a suite of measures intended to address an issue of concern for governments;

- aim to improve the human condition, raising the well-being of individuals and communities at risk;

- may struggle with overlapping plans and actions as vested interests and competing jurisdictions interpret place-based policy agendas in a multitude of ways;

- are transnational in their application, finding expression across nations and a broad range of governmental systems; and

https://doi.org/10.1080/2578711X.2020.1783893
© 2020 Andrew Beer, Fiona McKenzie, Jiří Blažek,
Markku Sotarauta and Sarah Ayres

- are not restricted to questions of the economy and economic performance; place-based policies can be found in many policy domains including public health and the delivery of social services.

To better understand place-based policies, we examined the governmental processes that underpin and shape these policies in order to identify the factors likely to lead to success or failure.

This Policy Expo looks at five case studies of place-based policy. The examples illustrate both the global ubiquity of place-based approaches and their capacity to be applied to a wide variety of challenges for public policy. The case studies also differed considerably in their scale and strategic intent. The policies implemented in the city of Iida (Japan) around energy generation and marine innovation in Nova Scotia (Canada) were implemented as a defensive strategy – preserving fishery resources and livelihoods in the latter instance, and the city population in the former. By contrast, the place-based polices of South Moravia (Czechia), on the one hand, and Sweden and Finland, on the other, were more forward-looking: mobilising local capacities to drive innovation and economic growth.

There was considerable variation in the origin of the policies. In Iida, a Japanese local government was the primary catalyst for innovation. In Gippsland (Victoria, Australia) and South Moravia, state or regional governments (or their semi-autonomous agencies) led the process of policy experimentation, while the Swedish Regional Growth through Dynamic Innovation Systems (VINNVÄXT) and Finnish Centre of Expertise (CoE) programmes reflected the ambitions and drivers of national governments, and their willingness to use both 'top-down' and 'bottom-up' processes to achieve their objectives.

The case studies present the rich variety that is place-based policy, but also several commonalities. One such thread is the importance of working across governments and in association with the broader community. In South Moravia, Gippsland as well as in Finland and Sweden, collaboration across the tiers of government and a spectrum of organisations was a central element of the policy design, while in Japan and Sweden, the investment decisions of civil society organisations and the private sector were critical to achieving programme objectives.

In all instances, polices were developed and implemented across a considerable timeframe with a 10-year horizon embedded in the framework of the VINNVÄXT programme and key to success in South Moravia. Finally, understanding what success looks like – a shift to sustainable energy and population levels in Japan; globally competitive industries in Finland; ongoing employment for affected workers in the Latrobe Valley of Gippsland – were all critical for defining each place-based policy.

At a broader level, the case studies highlighted the fact that place-based policies can be successful under a wide range of circumstances, with different systems of government, variable resourcing, diverse aims and objectives, and distinctive cultural contexts and economic systems. We concluded that it is the process of implementation that determines whether a place-based policy will achieve its goals. *Place-based policies require more than just high-quality policy-setting and programme design capacities: the nature, duration and collaborative approach used to bring them to life is critical.*

There can be no denying that there are significant impediments to the implementation of successful place-based policies, but for many parts of the contemporary global economy there is no alternative. As Rodríguez-Pose has observed, spatially blind policies have left too many places behind, resulting in political and economic uncertainty. The only solution is the implementation of place-based policies that can help every region, city, industry and community reach its potential.[1]

REFERENCE

1   Rodríguez-Pose A (2018) The revenge of the places that don't matter (and what to do about it). *Cambridge Journal of Regions, Economy and Society*, 11(1): 189–209.

KEY RECOMMENDATIONS

RECOMMENDATION 1

Governments around the globe need to develop better place-based policies because governmental frameworks that rely upon spatially blind policy settings simply will leave too many cities and regions behind.

Economic recession brought on by the impact of the COVID-19 pandemic needs to be addressed by a full portfolio of policies if we are to achieve both economic and social 'bounceback'.

RECOMMENDATION 2

Governments need to 'join the dots' and recognise that successful place-based policies are multidimensional, and programmes will be successful if they consider each of our 10 key determinants of success. We found the most effective place-based policies:

1. have, by definition, an explicit focus on place and are organised to make use of the full set of opportunities and resources in that locality;
2. recognise that an engagement with local institutions is central to achieving their mission;
3. focus on governance, accepting the need to create robust, sustainable and transparent processes and acknowledge the key role of erudite and charismatic leaders;
4. emphasise value creation and the local capture of value in order to generate opportunities in the short, medium and long terms;
5. acknowledge the need to consider the performance of places over a long timeframe;
6. are an important tool for targeting assistance to those individuals and groups for whom adjustment processes are most challenging;
7. accept that there is an emotional dimension to questions of place and the future of places: this may be especially evident in periods of rapid change – such as disruption to local industries – but is present in all circumstances;

https://doi.org/10.1080/2578711X.2020.1783895
© 2020 Andrew Beer, Fiona McKenzie, Jiři Blažek,
Markku Sotarauta and Sarah Ayres

8. incorporate outcome and output measures – qualitative and quantitative – early in the implementation of place-based initiatives in order to drive achievement;

9. avoid faltering expectations and a cycle of disillusionment by having demonstrable, significant, achievements built into the program' design: these can be short term, long term or developmental and need to be communicated to all stakeholders, including the wider community; and

10. embrace an explicit focus on the goals and aspirations of that specific place-based policy from inception, and these need to be agreed to by all stakeholders.

RECOMMENDATION 3

Governments need to recognise that how they implement place-based policy is as important – if not more important – than what is implemented.

Good-governance arrangements are essential if place-based policies and programmes are to achieve their goals. This means that arrangements that provide an oversight of such initiatives must include an appropriate mix of stakeholders, including those representative of disadvantaged groups as well as those with the power to bring about change through the organisations they lead or work within.

Many of these stakeholders have resources they can contribute to the shared objectives of specific place-based policies. Good governance calls for well-understood aims, but also transparent and robust processes around information-sharing and decision-making.

Individuals and groups within affected communities need to have access to decision-making and its associated power and responsibilities. Such arrangements are essential if there is to be a local 'buy in'.

RECOMMENDATION 4

Government agencies must acknowledge they cannot achieve their goals if they fail to take the community with them. Local leaders need to be an integral component of all place-based policy designs and implementation.

Their active involvement is essential in order to achieve the mobilisation of community resources, a long-term perspective, the patience to work towards goals in the distant future, and community acknowledgement of the value of such policies.

1. WHAT IS PLACE-BASED POLICY?

1.1 INTRODUCTION

Technological change, an aging work force and a global economic downturn are posing enormous challenges to OECD regions. While some regions are equipped to confront and handle these changes, others are struggling to remain competitive.[1]

As the Organisation for Economic Co-operation and Development (OECD) observed a decade ago, many regions in developed economies have struggled to reshape themselves in the face of rapid national and global economic change. The Barca Report, *An Agenda for a Reformed Cohesion Policy* (2009), firmly put place-based policy at the heart of the European agenda and elevated place-based policy on the global stage.[2] Many cities and regions have been called on to adjust their industry mix or the practices of their major industries as a consequence of environmental change, the rise of new technologies or the loss of a longstanding competitive advantage. Some cities and regions have been able to reshape themselves as local, national and global markets have changed, but others have found it a near impossible challenge as they have been 'locked' into particular development pathways. Place-based policies are one way that governments and institutions look to respond to economic and social challenges, bringing together a package of measures that seek to meet regional needs in their totality.

As the term implies, place-based policies have a focus on specific cities, localities or regions, but they represent far more than just a label for already established programmes of government activity, or the concentration of public sector resources in specific locations. Place-based policies embody an ethos about, and an approach to, the development of economies and society that acknowledges that the context of each and every city, region and rural district offers opportunities for advancing well-being. It advocates for a development approach tailored to the needs of each. Importantly, place-based policy explicitly seeks the development of all parts of the landscape, with no settlement too small or too remote to plan for progress (Figure 1.1).

Over the past decade increased attention has been paid to place-based policy-making. This focus has been evident in the European Union (EU) and several other nations and has been applied to a wide-range of policy domains, including the emergence of place-based leadership, industry policy, innovation, and in managing the impacts of economic shocks and economic transition. There are strong intersections with other areas of academic work, such as the literature on city and regional leadership.[3] There is also a growing movement towards place-focused industry policies.[4] Other areas of convergence include the development of industry clusters, the creation of entrepreneurial eco-systems, the implementation of Smart Specialisation and the development of spatially bound infra-structure programmes. Many or all of these initiatives can be identified as examples of place-based policy (Box 1.1).

https://doi.org/10.1080/2578711X.2020.1783897

Figure 1.1 Place-based policy: core elements

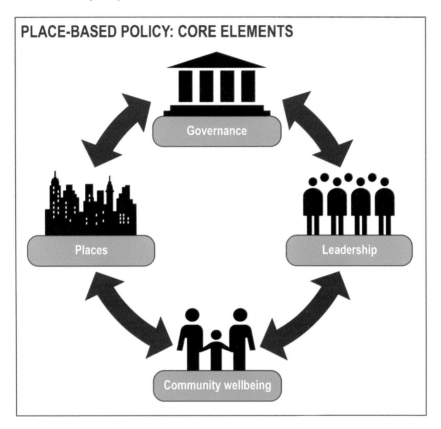

PLACE-BASED POLICY: CORE ELEMENTS

Governance

Places

Leadership

Community wellbeing

Box 1.1 What is place-based policy?

WHAT IS PLACE-BASED POLICY?

The project team was able to seek views of colleagues at the 2019 Regional Studies Association Annual Conference workshop in Santiago de Compostela. An opening question to the focus group discussion was "What do you think of when we say 'place-based policy'?" The responses to this question gives a sense of the broad and varied elements which may be included in the concept:

- Coordination of challenges
- Multiple levels of governance
- Collective public good
- Complex policy
- Smart specialisation
- Place leadership

- Shared leadership
- Consensus
- Cross-boundary
- Shared goal
- Community aims
- Co-design

- Social networks
- Social capital
- Links between actors
- Individual agency
- Local institutions

The origins of place-based policy may be traced to the 1990s.[5] That decade saw governments influenced by several influential thinkers, for example:

- Alan Scott showed how individual cities and regions can shape national economic growth through their influence on individual technologies.[6]

- Paul Krugman established 'the new economic geography' and showed the ways in which cities and regions linked trade to economic growth.[7]

- Michael Porter demonstrated how clusters of locally based industries were a driving force in national economies.[8]

- Ed Glaeser and colleagues set out how the characteristics of individual cities shape growth.[9]

- Adam Jaffe and colleagues articulated the important role of knowledge spillovers and exchange as a determinant of growth.[10]

While each of these authors made a distinctive contribution, their combined work provided the intellectual foundation and policy rationale for place-based policy.[11] The use of place-based policies by government was influenced by the impacts of globalisation which affected not only individuals but also places:

modern globalisation has increased the differences between places which are 'winners' and places which are 'losers' from globalization ... regions and cities which are dominated by multinational firms, internationally renowned universities, high quality and large scale research centres, high quality transportation and communications infrastructures, and highly qualified workforces, tend to be places which are prospering in the modern economy. ... In contrast, places with few of these assets or characteristics tend to be struggling and left behind in the modern economy in many ways.[12]

Overall, this body of work on 'place' and 'places' as a key determinant of economic success set the ground for new policy formulations. Alongside this was debate about the rising disenfranchisement of those living in the 'places that don't matter'.[13] The most notable initiative was the Barca Report mentioned above. It took the modernisation of the EU budget as its starting point, but concluded that place-based policy was the best possible solution to achieving the EU's economic and social goals. In the words of McCann, the Barca Report argued that:

tackling institutionally-generated policy traps was a critical priority and role for nationally-led regional policy. In particular, well designed and locally tailored regional policies which fostered the local engagement of many different types of (private, public and civil society) stakeholders could help to unlock development traps.[14]

In addition, Barca argued that place-based policies need to be a form of public intervention that relies on local knowledge, and that such interventions are 'superior to alternative strategies', especially in their capacity to address inefficiencies in the economy as well as persistent social exclusion.[15]

Despite the emergence of place-based policy, several authors have argued such initiatives lack conceptual clarity and operational precision.[16] Ironically, the Barca Report had called for 'greater coherence with the place-based or territorial policy concept'.[17] The subsequent lack of a shared understanding and agenda for action may partly be due to the ways in which the stakeholders within institutions have fundamentally reshaped their understanding of this concept, and their engagement with public debate on this issue, to best suit their own priorities. This brings with it two risks: first, the concept of place-based policy has run the risk of being diluted as it has been attached to a very broad range of very different policies and actions; and second, it has led to less effective strategies being adopted, in turn resulting in a sense of disillusionment and the abandonment of such interventions. Moreover, there is not a literature on 'best practice case studies' for place-based policies and associated transitions. There are several published case studies, but these do not represent a formal catalogue of successful policy implementation and are more likely to highlight the limitations and deficiencies evident in particular instances.

There are a number of complex issues relating to place-based policy, and there is a notable absence of clarity for public sector authorities charged with mapping out new place-based frameworks. There are questions around how to identify success factors and risks for the effective implementation of place-based policy, and there are also uncertainties around the *ex-ante* conditions that need to be in place for the successful implementation of place-based policy, that is, the circumstances and structures that provide fruitful ground for place-based policy. Importantly, researchers and policy-makers alike need to know more about the role of governance, and innovation in governance, as a pathway to the successful implementation of place-based policy. They also need to know how to both understand, and bring into positive effect, the capacities of communities and community leaders.

In short, there is a disconnect between academic writing in this field and the policy advice and prescriptions readily available to those charged with implementing development. There is an unquestioned need within policy networks and the community at large for stronger insights into 'what works' and what does not, with respect to place-based policy. Therefore, this Policy Expo addresses these gaps by drawing together insights from academics, policy-makers and the lessons learned from case studies of several place-based interventions.

1.2 DEFINING PLACE

Regions have formed a core concept in geographical thinking since the late 19th century, whereas place is a more recent addition to the geographical vocabulary.[18] Concepts of place and region overlap semantically in many ways, but each has its own history and meaning.[19] The term 'region' is a scalable concept that usually refers to a subnational scale, but may also be applied to a supranational scale such as the Baltic Sea Region or the Middle East Region.[20] In summary, a region should be homogeneous in terms of specified criteria, and these commonly include functional, administrative, cultural and/or social phenomena that can establish a narrative of similarity, demarcating one place from another. Although there has been a recent push for a refocus on regions as *functional* areas, many still argue that regions are better understood as territories endowed with some (self-) governing competence.[21] This is important in terms of the mobilisation of public support and design of policies.

A region should be distinguishable from bordering areas by an identifiable association of related features, industry structure, common history or other cultural links. Importantly, 'a region' does not have a determinate size, and in academic research a 'region' is simply an analytical concept, a focusing device, and should be defined for each and every piece of research. The borders of regions can and do change and reflect the decisions, actions and industry structures of that point in time. Borders are perhaps best thought of as semi-permeable – simultaneously both open and closed, depending on the social practices and discourses that construct and shape them.[22]

By contrast, the concept of place is a more subjective idea, and one that embraces both a sense of attachment and an emotional linkage. It involves a sense of belonging, a sense of presence and of being in an environment. Collinge et al.[23] suggest that the concept of place includes three dimensions:

- *location*: the fixed geographical coordinates of a physical location;
- *locale*: the material settings for social relations; and
- *the sense of place*: the subjective emotional attachment people have to places they inhabit.

Place emphasises human experience and subjective views on development and change. Significantly 'place' adds a human dimension and focus to studies of subnational phenomena. This is critical for place-based policy because it speaks to the motivations of individuals and groups. It draws our attention to a specific location, its institutional settings and meanings for people.

1.3 POLICY AND PLACE

The concept of policy leads us to narrow our focus to government efforts to shape the growth of places. Place-based policy directs our attention to public efforts to boost the development of cities and regions by taking into account peoples' values, local assets and knowledge, as well as locally derived visions and intentions.

A policy is a deliberately formulated system of principles and related objectives to guide decision-making and make it as rational as possible.[24] Public policies are defined and shaped in a political process. In the 21st century, the engagement in and contribution of various stakeholders is common to the policy-formation process, including community groups, higher education institutions and private sector actors. However, public policies remain primarily the domain of *governments* because they are made in the public's name, thus bringing the role and authority of government into sharp relief.[25] Policies are generally formulated or initiated by a government, even in cases with extensive participation of various societal groups. Importantly, a policy is not only what the government intends to do but also what it decides not to do.

Place-based policies assume that geography truly matters. Barca et al.[26] argued that local/regional development strategies should not be spatially blind and thus indifferent to the specificities of places, indifferent to geography. Moreover, space-neutral policies are never as neutral as assumed by their advocates; policies always have – intended or not – spatial effects. Place-based policies recognise that the institutions embedded within places, as well as locally embedded knowledge and action, are the appropriate cornerstones upon which to build local prosperity. As Bailey et al.[27] contended, there is a need for 'an integrative approach, with a mix of appropriate inclusive policies across a range of policy domains, reflecting the desired and aimed-for competitive advantage of regions'.

Jessop[28] has argued that the territorial organisation of political authority is the essential feature of modern statehood. It has different forms and rests on specific political, economic and relational attributes that result in different kinds of place-based governance arenas and leadership potentials.[29] He suggests that regions serve as policy laboratories for experimentation in government and governance, and these experiments have implications for redesigning institutions, policies and politics in response to policy failures and other crises. Indeed, there is a growing literature on so-called 'place-based' solutions to policy issues and problems.

1.4 PLACE-BASED VERSUS SPATIALLY BLIND POLICIES

A great deal of attention has been paid to the extent to which government interventions in the economy should be either place based or place neutral. Whilst place-neutral advocates promote the role of aspatial 'people-based' policies, place-based approaches highlight the importance of the interactions between place-based communities, institutions and geography, which requires researchers and policy-makers 'to explicitly consider the specifics of the local and wider regional context'.[30]

Place-based policy approaches and philosophies sit in contrast with other perspectives on how to grow economies and improve human well-being. One school of thought comes from a specific reading of neo-classical economics and argues that growth is predicated on free markets and minimal state intervention. Important advocates of this approach have included the World Bank,[31] which has argued that advocating for the growth of weaker regions comes at a cost to the national economy. Place-based policies, it has argued, have an uncertain track record in levelling development outcomes within and across nations. In addition, it argued that economic activity is inevitably 'lumpy', and policies should focus on the 'spatially blind provision of essential public services and balanced regulation of land, labour and product markets'.[32]

Academics have also argued against place-based or regional policies, contending they reduce competitiveness by discouraging industry from establishing in the most productive locations. Others suggest they too often result in infrastructure investment for which there is limited demand, and effectively represent the misallocation of scarce public sector resources. Similarly, the American urban economist Glaeser[33] has argued metropolises now dominate national and regional economies, and the goal of policy should be to facilitate and accelerate the role of cities as engines of growth.

Similar arguments have been made within nations. Taking some highly influential work in Australia as an example, the high-profile think tank the Grattan Institute set out to examine the economic development of Australian regions and whether regional development policies could increase growth rates in lagging regions in cost-effective ways. The institute adopted a narrow perspective on regional development and place-based policy, focusing solely on the economic development of regions, measured by growth in population, employment and average incomes. It limited its analysis of place-focused programmes and policies to infrastructure spending intended to assist disadvantaged regions, while a second line of enquiry considered programmes meant to assist workers and regions affected by plant closures and other shocks.[34] However, in dealing with what it called a 'patchwork economy', it came to the sobering conclusion that: 'the available evidence suggests that a government that attempts to even out regional economic growth rates is engaging in a futile exercise to push economic water uphill'.[35] The institute argued that 'a decade of special assistance for lagging regions, has not translated into sustainable economic growth',[36] and concluded that assistance should be focused on individuals, not regions or industries.

Advocates of place-based policies, of course, take a very different perspective, contending that approaches that have sometimes been labelled as 'spatial Keynesianism' are essential because of market failures and the profound regional differences in growth imperatives and opportunities. Opponents of 'spatially blind' policies have assembled convincing arguments in support of place-based policies as critical tools used in the delivery of national and regional well-being. The OECD analysed the growth of regions within its member states over a decade and concluded that spatially blind policies are a necessary, but not sufficient, condition for growth.[37] It found that while the 1990s were dominated by growth in the major cities, economic development moved away from the large metropolitan regions at the start of the 21st century. The OECD concluded nations have a clear need for spatially focused policies because economy-wide growth increasingly depends on the performance of lagging regions, as well as those growing strongly.

Advocates of place-based policy argue that a spatially decentralised political base can allow for differentiation in regional policies, and that policy should seek to encourage diversity and experimentation across regions.[38] In addition, the emergence of new actors at the subnational level creates opportunities for cross-border and international initiatives that, in turn, boost national economic growth. Indeed, there has been a recent abundance of academic and policy interest in place-based approaches for promoting economic productivity, generating creative policy responses and harnessing civic engagement.[39]

Critically, place-based policy and the associated actions by government are not just a matter of terminology or labels: they represent a specific philosophy of government, and a commitment to actions of a particular type and in a defined manner. The views of the two sides in this argument are diametrically opposed, with each advocating for very different policies and government actions. While several reviews have attempted to provide policy closure, the fundamental questions and value conflicts embedded within this debate remain unresolved. This debate is one of the 'big questions' in contemporary social science and economic policy formation, challenging our understanding of the relationship between regions and national economies. The key elements of this debate are summarised in Figure 1.2, which emphasises the competing values, goals and mechanisms of the two approaches.

Figure 1.2 Delivering economic growth: place-based versus spatially blind policies.

SPATIALLY-BLIND POLICIES
Leading advocate: World Bank 2009

- National focus
- Unfettered markets
- Labour mobility
- Large cities
- Resources are concentrated to drive technological innovation
- Dispersion of policies and expenditures seen as a risk for growth

PLACE-BASED POLICIES
Leading advocate: OECD

- City and region focus
- Strategic support for places
- Labour embeddedness
- Dispersed growth
- Resources focussed on growth for all
- Inequality seen as a risk for growth

Source: Rainnie et al. (2018), see Reference 40

It is possible to identify some form of rapprochement between the two perspectives, with a degree of repositioning evident. For example, the World Bank recently identified an important role for the capacities of government agencies and governance in areas such as human capital formation and the sharing of prosperity.[40] There has also been a growing acknowledgement that inequity, both spatial and individual, is an impediment to growth. Growth in the presence of inequality, it has recognised, generates what Ostry and Bourginon label as 'fragile' rather than the 'inclusive' growth.[41] Rainnie et al. suggested the spatial dimensions of this re-evaluation by the World Bank are likely to emerge more prominently.[42]

1.5 SUBJECTIVE ASPECTS OF PLACE-BASED POLICY

A focus on subjective issues – a sense of attachment to 'place', the question of 'regional policy for whom' and a focus on inclusion – is embedded in many of assessments of place-based policy. This focus on emotion and fairness is one of the defining features of place-based policy and, to a degree, differentiates it from earlier generations of policy interventions, such as area-based policy.

In the 21st century, well-informed place-based policy incorporates the subjective elements of regional embeddedness and future-making. Policies that ignore the emotion of economic change and job loss in the name of impartiality and rationality effectively turn their back on the dynamics through which individual lives are lived and societies are made.[43] Emotions are fundamental to meaning and identity; they are central to one's experience of identity and place.[44] A body of work argues that a strong local identity can be a powerful driver for place-based policy.[45]

The focus on emotion and feelings within place-based policy pays homage to the importance of places within the lives of individuals, families and communities. Regions and places unable to adjust to a new economic order see households and families separated, as individuals seek work elsewhere, and those who remain behind face lower incomes and living standards in a depressed local economy. Governments may struggle to provide services at an appropriate standard in such regions, and remaining businesses may face increased difficulty in securing the opportunities, labour and infrastructure they require. Good and effective place-based strategies therefore consciously build this element into the delivery and evaluation of the programme.

1.6 STRUCTURE OF THE BOOK

This Policy Expo explores the opportunities and challenges for governments when adopting a place-based policy approach. Following this opening chapter, the next chapter considers the potential benefits of adopting place-based approaches to policy. The third chapter looks at some of the factors deemed important to ensuring the success of place-based solutions, as well as some of the risks and challenges associated with them. The fourth chapter uses a series of case studies to show how real-world situations provide an insight into the benefits, characteristics and factors influencing place-based policy. Finally, the book concludes by arguing that place-based policies have the potential to enhance economic productivity, policy effectiveness and democracy. However, outcomes across the globe are variable and measurement is prone to distortion.

While there is no clear and consistent evidence on the link between place-based policy-making and policy effectiveness, the literature identifies a number of critical success factors that are shown to lead to both the success and failure of place-based policy solutions in particular circumstances. Governments and policy-makers around the world are advised to consider the relevance of these factors in their local areas when considering place-based policy options.

REFERENCES

1 Organisation for Economic Co-operation and Development (OECD) (2009) *Policy Brief: How Regions Grow*. March. Paris: OECD, p. 1.

2 Barca F (2009) *An Agenda for a Reformed Cohesion Policy*. Independent report to the Commissioner for Regional Policy. Brussels: European Union.

3 Sotarauta M (2016) *Leadership and the City: Power, Strategy and Networks in the Making of Knowledge Cities*. Abingdon: Routledge; Hambleton R (2015) Practice papers place-based leadership: A new perspective on urban regeneration. *Journal of Urban Regeneration and Renewal*, 9(1): 10–24.

4 Bailey D, Pitelis C and Tomlinson P (2018) A place-based developmental regional industrial strategy for sustainable capture and co-created value. *Cambridge Journal of Economics*, 42(6): 1521–1542. Rodríguez-Pose A and Wilkie C (2016) *Revamping Local and Regional Development through Place-Based Strategies*. Penn Institute for Urban Research,

Working Paper prepared for Reinventing Our Communities: Transforming Our Communities, Federal Reserve Bank of Philadelphia, Biennial Conference, September.

5 McCann, P (2019) *UK Research and Innovation: A Place-Based Shift?* UK Research and Innovation.

6 Scott A (1988) *New Industrial Spaces*. London: Pion.

7 Krugman P (1989) Differences in income elasticities and trends in real exchange rates. *European Economic Review*, 33(5): 1031–1046. Krugman P (1991) *Geography and Trade*. Cambridge, MA: MIT Press.

8 Porter M (1990) *The Competitive Advantage of Nations*. New York: Free Press.

9 Glaeser E, Kallal H, Scheinkman J and Shleifer A (1992) Growth in cities. *Journal of Political Economy*, 100(6): 1126–1152.

10 Jaffe A, Trajtenberg M and Henderson R (1993) Geographic localisation of knowledge spillovers as evidenced by patent citations. *Quarterly Journal of Economics*, 108(3): 577–598.

11 McCann (2019), p. 8, see Reference 5.

12 McCann (2019), pp. 9–10, see Reference 5.

13 Rodríguez-Pose A (2018) The revenge of the places that don't matter (and what to do about it). *Cambridge Journal of Regions, Economy and Society*, 11(1): 189–209.

14 McCann (2019), p. 11, see Reference 5.

15 Barca (2009), p. vii, see Reference 2.

16 Pugalis L and Bentley G (2014) Place-based development strategies: Possibilities, dilemmas and ongoing debates. *Local Economy*, 29(4–5): 561–572, at 563. Horlings L, Roep D and Wellbrock W (2018) The role of leadership in place-based development and building institutional arrangements. *Local Economy*, 33(3): 245–268.

17 Barca (2009), p. viii, see Reference 2.

18 Paasi A, Harrison J and Jones M (2018) New consolidated regional geographies. In A Paasi, J Harrison and M Jones (eds.), *Handbook on the Geographies of Regions and Territories*, pp. 1–20. Cheltenham: Edward Elgar.

19 Entrikin N (2018) Geography of experience: place and region. In A Paasi, J Harrison and M Jones (eds.), *Handbook on the Geographies of Regions and Territories*, pp. 44–45. Cheltenham: Edward Elgar.

20 Paasi et al. (2018), see Reference 18.

21 Cooke P, Urrunga M and Etxebarria G (2011) Regional innovation systems: Institutional and organisational dimensions. *Research Policy*, 26(4–5): 475–491.

22 Paasi A and Zimmerbauer, K (2016) Penumbral borders and planning paradoxes: Relational thinking and the questions of borders in spatial planning. *Environment and Planning A*, 48(1): 75–93.

23 Collinge C, Gibney J and Mabey C (2011) *Leadership and Place*. Abingdon: Routledge.

24 Parsons W (1995) *Public Policy: An Introduction to the Theory and Practice of Policy Analysis*. Aldershot: Edward Elgar.

25 Birkaland T (2016) *An Introduction to the Policy Process: Theories, Concepts, and Models of Public Policy Making*. Abingdon: Routledge, p. 20.

26 Barca F, McCann P and Rodríguez-Pose A (2012) The case for regional development intervention: Place-based versus place-neutral approaches. *Journal of Regional Science*, 52(1): 134–152, at 139.

27 Bailey D, Pitelis C and Tomlinson P (2018) A place-based developmental regional industrial strategy for sustainable capture and co-created value. *Cambridge Journal of Economics*, 42(6): 1521–1542, at 17.

28 Jessop B (2016) Territory, politics, governance and multispatial metagovernance. *Territory, Politics, Governance*, 4(1): 8–32, at 14. doi:10.1080/21622671.2015.1123173

29 Beer A and Clower T (2014) Mobilising leadership in cities and regions. *Regional Studies Regional Science*, 1(1): 4–18.

30 Barca et al. (2012), p. 140, see Reference 26.

31 World Bank (2009) *World Development Report 2009 – Reshaping Economic Geography*. Washington, DC: World Bank.

32 Gill I (2010) Regional development policies: place-based or people centred. *Vox*, October, 3.

33 Glaeser E (2012) *Triumph of the City*. New York: Penguin.

34 Bailey et al. (2018), see Reference 27; Rodríguez-Pose and Wilkie (2016), see Reference 4.

35 Daley J and Lancy A (2011) *Investing in Regions: Making a Difference*. Melbourne: Grattan Institute, p. 6.

36 Daley and Lancy (2011), p. 26, see Reference 35.

37 Organisation for Economic Co-operation and Development (OECD) (2009) *How Regions Grow: Trends and Analysis*. Paris: OECD; OECD (2012) *Promoting Growth in All Regions*. Paris: OECD.

38 Gibb A (1993) Key factors in the design of policy support for the small and medium enterprise (SME) development process: an overview. *Entrepreneurship and Regional Development*, 5(1): 1–24.

39 Martin R, Tyler P, Storper M, Evenhuis E and Glasmeier A (2018) Globalization at a critical conjuncture? *Cambridge Journal of Regions, Economy and Society*, 11(1): 3–16; Bailey D, Lyall S and Wood M (2015) *Democracy: The Missing Link in the Devolution Debate*. London: New Economics Foundation.

40 World Bank (2018) *Building Trust in Government through Citizen Engagement*. Washington, DC: World Bank.

41 Ostry J and Bourguignon F (2016) Inequality and the fragility of growth. In K Basu and J Stiglitz (eds.), *Inequality and Growth: Patterns and Policy*, pp. 136–162. London: International Economics Association, Palgrave Macmillan.

42 Rainnie A, Beer A and Rafferty M (2018) *Effectiveness of Place-Based Packages: Preliminary Framework Report*. Canberra: Regional Australia Institute, p. 6.

43 Anderson A and Smith S (2001) Editorial: Emotional geographies. *Transactions of the Institute of British Geographers*, 26(1): 7–10, at 7.

44 Pini B, Mayes R and McDonald P (2010) The emotional geography of a mine closure: A study of the Ravensthorpe nickel mine in Western Australia. *Social and Cultural Geography*, 11(6): 559–574.

45 Wills J (2016) (Re)locating community in relationships: Questions for public policy. *Sociological Review*, 64(4): 639–656.

2. WHAT ARE THE BENEFITS OF PLACE-BASED POLICY?

2.1 INTRODUCTION

Place-based policy approaches have the potential to make a significant contribution to communities across several policy domains, including the promotion of innovation, the development of local leadership capacities and in managing significant economic transitions. Some of the goals of place-based policy-making are to foster the growth of local economies, increase the efficiency of public services, and improve the legitimacy and accountability of political institutions by fostering political participation amongst citizens. Indeed, nations and regions around the world have been implementing spatial reforms in distinct and unique ways. Such restructuring is viewed by commentators as a response to a variety of pressures, including managing distinct national identities and cultures, accommodating economic diversity, relieving the political and bureaucratic burden associated with centralisation, and changing political views on the contribution of place-based policies to improve economic and social policies

2.2 GENERATING ECONOMIC GROWTH

2.2.1 Innovation and place-based policy

A great deal of research and writing places innovation – and specifically the promotion and facilitation of new technologies – in a central position with respect to place-based policy. This emphasis is unsurprising given that innovation and the promotion of technological advances now lie at the centre of most contemporary discussion of economic growth and development.[1] Innovation is seen to be both the key to productivity growth and the development of new industries with the capacity to sustain nations, cities and rural areas. Both are critical, with Nobel Laureate Paul Krugman observing that: 'Productivity growth isn't everything, but in the long term it's almost everything.'[2]

Many have discussed the importance of the regional scale for innovation, with authors such as Phil Cooke, Kevin Morgan and Björn Asheim publishing extensively on 'regional innovation systems' and associated processes.

Put simply, many place-based policies acknowledge that the best way to secure the long-term well-being of a region or city is to promote innovation in order to increase the viability of established industries and enterprises, while also encouraging the formation and growth of new businesses and technologies.

In consequence, one of the challenges for place-based policy is to establish new pathways that encourage innovation in order to enable the construction of a new regional future.

Metcalfe and Miles[3] examined the processes of innovation and argued that the 'restless' nature of contemporary economies and the uncertainty confronting businesses and places alike means that experimentation is a necessity. They saw innovation and its commercialisation as:

https://doi.org/10.1080/2578711X.2020.1783898

characterised by four features; the synthesis of ideas from different disciplines; the overwhelming impor-tance of the context of the application in shaping the process of collaboration in knowledge production; the great diversity of organisations (including firms) that contribute to solving problems ... and, the greater role of criteria external to science in determining the incentives to, and assessment of, the resulting outputs.[4]

From this perspective there is a clear need for policy to concentrate on establishing spaces for innovation rather than concentrating on specific innovations, and it is in these spaces that connections are formed between 'knowing' individuals and organisations.

Metcalfe and Miles distinguished between innovation systems and innovation ecologies, arguing that multiple innovation systems can be supported by a single, powerful, ecology. From this perspective, inno-vation ecologies are the set of individuals working within organisations who are the repositories and generators of new knowledge, and the 'system-making' connections that ensure the flow of information. This encompasses universities and firms that generate and store knowledge, as well as intermediaries who function as brokers. Innovation systems are part of the ecology, and are focused on finding a solution to particular innovation problems.

Ecosystems are also critical in allowing individual firms to succeed: Jarvi and Kortelainen[5] noted that while Nokia was able to succeed through its own efforts with the launch of its first mobile phone, further evolution of that product required development by content providers and in the supply of infra-structure. The failure of these supporting elements to succeed acted as a barrier to Nokia's continued success (Box 2.1).

Box 2.1   The complexity of innovation

Bessant et al.[33] argued there are now several core concepts underlying the promotion and management of innovation. These insights include the fact that:

- innovation is a process not an event;
- innovation management is a learning process;
- innovation is a spectrum of novelty;
- there are multiple pathways through the innovation space;
- creativity and problem solving are core disciplines;
- innovation inevitably involves entrepreneurship; and
- innovations are path dependent.

Critically, the promotion of innovation is acknowledged as one of the tasks confronting policy-makers and communities as they seek to reposition their economies within the global marketplace. *Place-based policies that ignore productivity and viability of the economy are most unlikely to deliver long-term success.*

2.2.2 Universities and place-based policy

Higher education institutions (HEIs), most commonly universities, are embedded in place-based policy designs. They frequently seek to be involved in shaping the future of their region, and they often present themselves to governments as the organisations best able to advance the knowledge economy in disadvantaged regions. Universities now carry a wide array of expectations:

- Their teaching is expected to enhance human capital for the modern economy.
- Their research seeks to maximise financial returns through commercialisation, profit-making, technology and innovation.
- They are often expected to engage with local businesses and communities to enhance local capacities for economic expansion while raising competitiveness.

At a fundamental level, many assumptions about economic development were challenged between the 1970s and 1990s as the developed world de-industrialised. Newly emerging industries in information technology and the biosciences were characterised by close links with science, technology and knowledge inputs. The development of new centres of economic activity in the global market, for example, Silicon Valley, and health sciences in places such as San Diego, showed the economic value of high-technology development and research coming together in specific locations. Across the Organisation for Economic Co-operation and Development (OECD) and in many developing nations, formal regional development policy shifted from top-down national government intervention to neoliberal models of development that placed a greater focus on the local. The promotion and provision of assistance to small and medium-sized enterprises in order to enhance innovation became important elements in new approaches to boosting competitiveness. In this mindset of economic development, the regional, rather than national, scale became significant, and there was an emerging focus on the capacity of networks in the global economy to cut across national boundaries.

Economic theory has changed its view of the factors affecting economic growth, particularly in relation to human capital, notably education levels and the generation of knowledge. Economic models have made giant strides forward in their capacity to explain where economic growth occurs and where it does not through a new focus on human capital. In the endogenous economic growth theories of both Lucas and Romer,[6] human capital becomes a key *driver* of technological progress through innovation and creativity. Lucas subsequently argued that investment in, and accumulation of, knowledge has benefits for many firms across the economy.

Higher education has become important to the performance of the economy: as a source of skilled labour/personnel, as the fountainhead of technological innovation and as part of the global branding of cities and regions. The capacity of universities to supply skilled labour is seen as one of the most important contributions they can make as know-how and skills of the workforce have taken on an increasingly central role in economic success.

Universities form a significant nexus in modern economic development because of their role in knowledge generation. They also have a potential role in directly stimulating national economic growth through their generation of higher skill levels and ability to connect localities to global knowledge flows. They are centrally placed in concepts such as the learning economy,[7] the learning region[8] and the triple helix.[9] The triple helix thesis sees the university as having an enhanced role in innovation within knowledge-based societies and economic growth processes, alongside business and government. The triple helix concept is one that is dynamic and reflexive, thus enhancing innovative potential though complex collaborations.[10]

Because universities have an important part to play in knowledge generation and dissemination, their role within endogenous regional growth theory is significant. They are not just providers of education or conductors of research, but also have a wider role, which includes generating and attracting talent, collaborating with local business, and facilitating innovation, entrepreneurship and competitiveness (Figure 2.1).

Figure 2.1   How universities contribute to regional growth

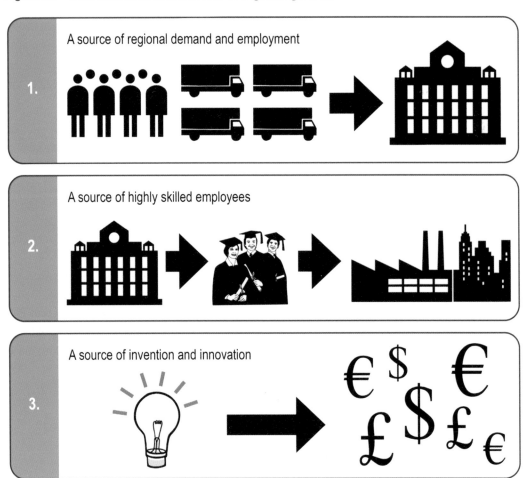

Universities are beneficial to local economies in terms of local income and employment multipliers; however, other processes may militate against such benefits. Economic growth is affected by the *mobility* of human capital produced by universities. Having gained education and skills, individuals are more likely to be mobile, especially given the opportunities in a global economy. This mobility diffuses the local impacts of the university as the benefits of their activity are spread over a much wider scale. Hence, the relationship between universities and local economic growth is not a simple one. Universities may contribute to a brain drain as graduates leave for opportunities unavailable locally.

This entrepreneurial role of universities has also reflected changes in the policy world. As centralised government planning processes were challenged in the 1970s by economic shocks such as the oil crisis and stagflation, moves towards a more neoliberal and competitive approach to government took hold, especially in the 1980s. Under these policy influences, universities were asked to become more competitive, entrepreneurial and to contribute to – or generate – their own funding.

Their capacity to contribute teaching and research outputs for an economy increasingly based on knowledge and human capital has given higher education institutions greater pre-eminence, and visibility, in economic planning and government-development strategies. They are often expected to play an important and deliberate role in driving economic growth. At the same time, universities have been expected to contribute to regional development. This can involve generating locally useful knowledge through research and also by working in partnership with local businesses to enhance their competitive position. They can play a role in regional capacity-building in more disadvantaged regions.

Overall, universities have emerged as a key component of place-based policies – whether they are policies implemented to deal with an economic shock, boost workforce capacities or raise the productivity of firms. Universities have taken on complex, multidimensional roles that reflect the aims and objectives of place-based policy, broadly defined.

2.3 CREATING BETTER POLICY OUTCOMES

Place-based policies offer the prospect of boosting economy-wide growth, but they are also called upon by governments to deal with apparently intractable social and economic challenges. In one sense, place-based policy is commonly applied as the solution of last resort. Examples include:

- The investments of the German government in regions affected by the long-term transition out of coal-mining.

- Australian government programmes boosting local and regional economies affected by the closure of the automotive industry.[11]

- The Finnish government's Abrupt Structural Change programme that supports regions being hit by globalisation and changes in production structures.

- Tn the UK, the Tony Blair New Labour government's introduction of 'targeted interventions to stabilize distressed neighbourhoods'.[12]

To a degree, the European Union's focus on 'Smart Specialisation' also represents a place-based solution to a challenge of public policy, in this instance the failure of European economies to demonstrate the levels of innovation and productivity growth evident in parts of the United States.

The capacity of place-based policy to offer solutions when other policy prescriptions have failed is a common theme within both the academic literature and in policy implementation. Barber,[13] for example, asserts that in the face of considerable global challenges, the nation-states of the world are paralysed. He claims that cities, and the mayors who run them, offer the best new drivers of good governance. Cities are home to more than half the world's population, a proportion of which will continue to grow. They are the primary incubator of the cultural, social and political innovations that shape our planet. Most importantly, they are unburdened by the issues of borders and sovereignty which hobble the capacity of nation-states to work with one another.[14]

Barber demonstrates that regardless of city size or political affiliation, local executives exhibit a non-partisan and pragmatic style of place-based governance that is lacking in national and international halls of power. Through these qualities of leadership, mayors are able to retain the trust of citizens in their office, help cities become beacons of good governance and spearhead city-to-city collaborations in order to better address shared problems. Barber's boldest proposal is a 'World Parliament of Mayors', established on a voluntary basis to enable cities to have a stronger voice in global affairs, provide a world-wide platform for the sharing and transfer of urban best practices, and establish a more democratic basis for addressing global priorities than has ever existed.

In a similar vein, Hambleton[15] argues that imaginative place-based policy can shape more inclusive, democratic and sustainable places. Drawing on detailed 'innovative stories' from around the globe, Hambleton describes how effective place-based policies can lead to policy innovation and impact. Examples include advances in the use of information and communication technology in Chicago, Illinois; dealing with troubled families in the UK; the provision of housing in South Africa; and city development in Auckland, New Zealand. Finally, renowned sociologist Anthony Giddens[16] has argued that the city level is the most effective scale from which to tackle challenging issues, such as environmental policy and climate change. He asserts that civic interest, engagement and action can be garnered and coordinated by local place-based leaders, and that global city leaders can work together more readily than nation-states. In this view, subnational leaders can engage in place-based policy to tackle difficult global and local challenges.[17]

Issues of complexity, stakeholder management, community engagement, uncertainty over policy impact and the diffusion of outcomes across a region present significant risks for place-based policy as part of the portfolio of activities in which governments engage. *Place-based programmes* are potentially vulnerable to the sorts of critiques put forward by advocates of the spatially blind policies discussed in chapter 1. They *remain part of the policy landscape, however, because of the failure of other forms of public sector or community action to achieve the aspirations of the community. In one sense, there is no alternative to place-based policy*, but this does not make the implementation or development of such policies more straightforward.

2.4 IMPROVING WELL-BEING

At its core, place-based policies seek to invest in, and improve, cities and regions in order to enhance the well-being of individuals and families. They look to raise incomes and quality of life by making individuals job ready, by bringing employment into the region or providing the infrastructure needed to connect to the global marketplace. Fundamentally they are concerned with improving the human condition – broadly conceived. This wide-ranging perspective on well-being means contemporary place-based policies incorporate subjective components of quality of life into their programme design. They are not simply limited to a conventional economic perspective; instead, they actively engage with a wide array of goals, and associated performance metrics.

It can be argued that the evaluation and analysis of place-based policies needs to take a multifaceted perspective on well-being. Place-based policies – unlike spatially blind policies – carry with them the potential to generate benefits for affected communities that span several policy domains and diverse determinants of individual and collective welfare.[18] In many ways they both seek to generate positive 'externalities' and exploit them in order to achieve their broader goals. For example, policies that raise female participation in the labour force in low-income regions are likely to:

- raise household incomes;

- improve educational outcomes;

- attract additional enterprises seeking that pool of labour; and

- add to the vibrancy of local retailers.

Good place-based policies need to incorporate a breadth of measures in order to advance our understanding of the impact they have had on the target community. Drawing on work by the OECD,[19] Tomaney also noted that 'much of the information required to design and implement a wellbeing strategy is found locally … [and] people generally assess their own sense of well-being based on their immediate socio-economic context'.[20]

Regional development scholars, as well as policy-makers and practitioners, are engaged in lively debates on new ways to advance the well-being and growth of individual places and groups of places. From 2010 to the present, place-based policy approaches and their incarnations – including Smart Specialisation – have dominated many of these efforts (for more on Smart Specialisation, see chapter 3, section 2).

2.5 RESPONDING TO ECONOMIC SHOCKS AND SUPPORTING TRANSITION

Place-based policies are commonly deployed – amongst other measures – by governments seeking to overcome, or reduce, the negative impacts of large-scale economic shocks, such as the closure of a major employer, or the demise of an entire industry (examples include the automotive industry in Australia and the German coal industry). These changes commonly result in substantial job losses, which generate long-term joblessness as cities and regions struggle with a sluggish local economy, significant numbers of unemployed workers with skills no longer sought by enterprises, low household incomes and an entrenched image of disadvantage. Governments frequently use a mix of income support, labour market training, health promotion and industry-development policies to address these challenges[21] with place-based policies applied to often difficult-to-define community impacts, while also stimulating growth.

Over recent decades a new focus has emerged within the policy-making landscape as the trade union movement has sought to step beyond its historical position of representing its members until they leave the industry. Instead, it has begun to actively advocate for 'Just Transitions'. Previously, workers forced out of employment were often denied access to a political, social and economic support network that had been a central pillar of their lives. Unions in Germany and elsewhere have come to appreciate the inequity and risks associated with this stance. Change in the world of work is ongoing and inescapable, especially in the face of industrial change necessitated by the need to move away from high carbon-emitting activities towards those with zero or low-carbon emissions.

In 2014, the ambitions and achievements of the Just Transitions movement were explored in a special issue of the *International Journal of Labour Research*, with this work reviewed by Rainnie et al.[22] The editors examined international examples of attempts to achieve a *Just Transition*, which they characterised as policies and programmes that acknowledged:

> both the opportunities for the creation of decent work in the transition to environmentally and socially sustainable economies and the challenges they represent. They underscore the critical role of governments, employers and workers as agents of change – individually and collectively.[23]

They held out the example of the Ruhr Valley in Germany as an exemplar of Just Transitions, noting that:

> The scope and reach of this transition, and its spread over time, make this experience unique, but also inspiring when we imagine the ways in which other regions in the world could similarly transform themselves. Clearly retirement, compensations for income loss, and wage subsidies for the reintegration of the unemployed and those threatened by unemployment, co-determination with employers and trade unions playing a critical – and responsible – role, and the list goes on: this example shows us the challenges ahead but also makes clear that it is indeed possible to transform a territory and preserve the environment while at the same time developing jobs and the economy.[24]

Snell[25] examined whether a Just Transition is a realistic prospect for parts of Australia affected by the closure of the brown coal industry. He observed that the concept of a '*Just Transition* has become an increasingly popular concept used to draw attention to the equity and justice challenges associated with efforts to steer society towards a more ecologically sustainable path',[26] and that it has been taken up by a wide range of academic commentators and international organisations, such as the International Labour Organisation (ILO). However, this success has resulted in:

a considerable divergence in views and interpretations of the concept … questions have been raised as to whether Just Transition is achievable or is simply aspirational, with the number of practical examples of successful instances of Just Transition remaining sparse and largely undocumented.[27]

Snell went on to suggest six key lessons could be drawn from the efforts to put a Just Transition into practice in the Latrobe Valley of Victoria:

- Unions need to take a proactive role through all stages of the transition process, and build their capacity in order to achieve this.

- There is a need to move beyond a narrow focus on the impact of government environmental policy on workers and their communities and also consider the impacts of the environmental policies of private firms.

- A Just Transition calls for unions and regional authorities to engage in both strategic planning for the future and an ongoing social dialogue.

- Unions, government, employers and community organisations need to collaborate if they are to achieve a Just Transition. Coalition-building is a common theme in the literature on this topic.

- Just Transition requires unions to innovate and move beyond the traditional industrial model of unionism they have performed when confronted by closures.

- The real test of Just Transition is the success of disadvantaged workers in finding decent work and the ability to keep families and communities intact. Unfortunately, evidence suggests that the ability for workers to find alternative decent employment after a closure is constrained. Just Transition, therefore, requires a long-term commitment to regional and employment revitalisation.

The effort to introduce a Just Transition into the Latrobe Valley provides a clear example of the way place-based policies commonly call on a range of actors from civil society, government and the community at large. It also highlights the need for a long-term commitment to improving the well-being of a place or set of places, and the ways that efforts intersect with other governmental and societal agendas – including moving to a sustainable economy. Finally, it is important to note how the Latrobe Valley has been the target of government efforts to introduce both Smart Specialisation strategies, as well as union and community-led measures designed to implement a Just Transition.

This multiplicity of effort speaks to both the flexibility of place-based policies and also the potentially for overlap, confusion and the perception of programmes of implementation that are partial and ineffective.

This observation brings to life the comments made around how the 'fuzzy' boundaries and ambitions around place-based policy can lead to poor outcomes and limited public support. For example, in 2017, the Australian government's Productivity Commission examined the transitions of regions undergoing profound change. Its starting proposition was that governments cannot, and should not, shield individuals and communities from all possible adverse events or ongoing pressures. However, it conceded that, on occasion, the existing social security, tax, training and job services systems are insufficient, and without further government intervention, the most vulnerable households and regions experience such severe, pervasive and persistent change that there is a strong likelihood of permanent disadvantage. It accepted that under these circumstances there is a case for additional support. When assistance is provided, it should:

- facilitate change for affected individuals;

- be targeted at those groups for whom adjustment pressures are the greatest;

- be transparent, both in policy and administration, and should also be of limited duration;

- mobilise and enfranchise local leaders; and

- be compatible with the general safety net arrangements.[28]

In Australia, such place-focused programmes of assistance are commonly referred to as structural adjustment programmes and they can take a number of forms depending upon governmental objectives, the problems that require solution, the nature of the affected region and the scale of challenge. Structural adjustment programmes generally have four dimensions: labour markets, compensation, industry and community. Beer[29] identified four types of structural adjustment programme, each of which has an explicit, or implicit, place focus (Box 2.2):

Box 2.2 Illawarra case study

Wollongong in New South Wales, Australia, is a city of approximately 180,000 that sits in the Illawarra region, 70 km south of Sydney. Its economy has long been dominated by a steel-making plant established at Port Kembla by BHP in the first decades of the 20th century. The city's economy is affected by its proximity to Sydney, with approximately 20,000 workers commuting to Sydney. The University of Wollongong is a significant economic force within the region, with students attracted from Sydney, southern New South Wales and internationally.

The steel industry at Port Kembla has been restructuring since the 1980s, with employees laid off and new technologies introduced to achieve greater efficiencies. In the 1990s, BHP restructured, spinning off Bluescope Steel (Port Kembla) and OneSteel (Whyalla) as separate businesses. In 2011, Bluescope announced a further 800 voluntary redundancies. In July 2011, the Australian government announced the A$30 million Illawarra Region Innovation and Investment Fund (IRIIF) to assist the region's economy adjust to a smaller manufacturing sector.

Discussions with stakeholders found a range of opinions on restructuring in the Illawarra and the roll out of the IRIIF. Some of the key points included:

- A sense that the IRIIF was implemented and closed too quickly, which meant that good projects were not put forward as they could not be fully developed in the available time.

- Some businesses that received IRIIF support subsequently suffered under the global financial crisis (GFC), but generally projects were considered appropriate and worthy of investment.
- Workers who were made unemployed sought comparable well-paid employment, especially in mining and related employment. Many were willing to participate in fly-in-fly-out work schedules, but few were willing to leave permanently for employment in anything other than mining.
- There was a strong sense that it was difficult to determine the impacts of the IRIIF investment, but several stakeholders felt the Australian government could have done more to keep them informed.
- Several stakeholders felt a greater level of control should have been devolved to local leaders, and there was a need for greater transparency in decision-making.

Other key insights included:

- An acknowledgement that many experienced – and well-paid – workers simply left the workforce.
- Those workers with skills in demand found employment easily, while others struggled.
- Workers benefitted from advice and training on how to apply for work.
- Many who remained in the region found employment at much lower wage levels.

Not all commentators agreed with the direction and pace of structural adjustment in the region. One noted that building high-quality infrastructure investment would enable a far stronger growth dynamic in the region, while others felt funding under the IRIIF was spread too thinly. All agreed it was important that the Australian government had been 'seen to act'.

- Industry restructuring programmes: designed to make an industry overall more efficient and sustainable in future by assisting the exit of industry participants (businesses) at risk of not being viable.

- Enterprise assistance programmes: designed to assist an industry by helping individual businesses remain active and competitive within the global marketplace.

- Labour market programmes: assist affected workers to find new employment.

- Inward investment strategies: build a new future for regions and/or compensate the community for the loss of economic opportunity.

In Australia, structural adjustment packages are place-based policy on a large scale: Beer found the Australian government committed some A$88 billion to such schemes over the period 2000–12. Despite this extensive experience, there is little evidence on the contribution they made to the well-being of affected individuals, cities and regions. In part this reflects the earlier discussion around the broader challenges of measuring and communicating the impact of place-based policies.

The available evidence suggests the success of these structural adjustment programmes is dependent on the assembly of the most appropriate mix of policy measures, including infrastructure provision, labour market assistance, education and training, inward investment, improved governance arrangements to facilitate economic activity, and place marketing. There is, it would appear, no guaranteed formula for success. On the other hand, it is clear that high-achieving structural adjustment programmes in Australia have a focus on people and place. Such place-based approaches have been described as a paradigm shift not only in articulating and comprehending urban development dynamics but also in the form and nature of development strategies.[30]

2.6 ADDRESSING DISADVANTAGE

Place-based policies fundamentally acknowledge that the challenges confronting households living in localities marked by entrenched disadvantage cannot be solved by the provision of individual level assistance alone. Instead, conventional labour market and income support programmes need to be complemented by government actions and strategies that improve economic conditions in the region as a whole, generating employment and income growth across the community. Such programmes, of course, represent a significant, and much more complex, departure from government programmes focused on individual workers or industries. They seek to recruit the capacities and investment (financial, political, human and intellectual) of a wide array of stakeholders, and this brings with it risks as well as rewards. In seeking to address the locality-wide determinants of well-being, place-based policies and interventions commonly involve actions whose outcomes are either difficult to assess, or only emerge over the long term.

In 2016, the Victorian Council of Social Service (VCOSS), which is an Australian-based not-for-profit organisation that advocates for social justice and the provision of social services, outlined its approach to place-based policy. It argued that an approach that identifies place in terms of the true boundaries of a community is important to the success of spatially informed policies and associated transition packages. VCOSS argued that a well-developed policy (and associated actions) needs to integrate an economic focus with attention to social considerations and a focus on the local scale. It considered it important those within the 'place' identify themselves as a community, but in some programmes a community's boundaries do not correspond with governmental demarcations. The 'place' may be smaller than a local government's borders, and *policies should prioritise the 'place' or community that has meaning for residents rather than the most convenient administrative unit*.

VCOSS, as an agency primarily focused on advocacy for better social services, argued that services and service provision was central to place-based policy. Many critical place-based initiatives are located on a service site (e.g., school or early childhood centre) and serve the local community connected to that service (i.e., service users and their families). Finally, the VCOSS perspective on place-based policy and its implementation prioritised coordination and integration, and it did so under the slogan 'One place, one plan'. VCOSS argued that to bring the community together, it is important to develop a single approach rather than attempt to bring to life several 'place-based' initiatives in the same location, sometimes with competing objectives. The manner in which place-based policy has been defined by VCOSS reflects the type of comprehensive definition needed by policy-makers and researchers alike.

Place-based policies offer much to governments and localities affected by decline and at risk of being overtaken by shifts in global markets. Place-based policies – by definition – will have highly variable outcomes, as needs and aspirations differ from place to place, and as strategies tailor-made to the needs of individual localities are implemented. Rodríguez-Pose and Wilkie[31] acknowledged this variability between sites with respect to the capabilities, resources and influence needed to make the most of place-based strategies. Nevertheless, they concluded that place-based strategies:

> are off to a promising start and that maximising the returns of place-based territorial development at the local level can be achieved via both (i) capacity building to ensure that localities and communities are technically capable of assuming the responsibilities associated with greater powers and developing territorially-oriented approaches and interventions, and (ii) the promotion of multilevel governance to enhance vertical and horizontal coordination, guaranteeing a sufficient degree of coherence between the resources allocated to, and responsibilities assumed, at local level and also minimal overlap between the actions taken by various tiers of government.[32]

2.7 CONCLUSIONS

This chapter has examined placed-based policy as a form of public policy, one of a potential suite of measures available to governments, and part of the apparatus and agenda-setting of the political process. It has been noted that place-based policies can be both proactive in their remit, through a focus on innovation, or reactive, as when they are used to respond to economic disruption. As policy instruments, they reflect a qualitatively different philosophy of the role of government, and the dynamics of contemporary economies, when compared with spatially blind policy settings. Place-based policies are not the exclusive domain of governments, with other actors – including universities – both contributors to, and stakeholders in, the use of such policies. The chapter has shown that place-based policies:

- are often applied as one part of a suite of measures intended to address an issue of concern for governments;

- aim to improve the human condition, raising the well-being of individuals and communities at risk;

- may struggle with overlapping plans and actions as vested interests and competing jurisdictions interpret place-based policy agendas in a multitude of ways;

- are transnational in their application, finding expression across nations and a broad range of governmental systems; and

- are not restricted to questions of the economy and economic performance – place-based policies can be found in many policy domains including public health the delivery of social services etc.

REFERENCES

1   Chester K (2018) The future of work: Is it something completely different? Paper presented at the Committee for the Economic Development of Australia, 17 July.

2   Krugman P (1997) *The Age of Diminished Expectations*. Boston: MIT Press, p. 24.

3   Metcalfe J and Miles I (2012) *Innovation Systems in the Service Economy: Measurement and Case Study Analysis*. Economics of Science, Technology and Innovation. Springer.

4   Metcalfe and Miles (2012), p. 12, see Reference 3.

5   Jarvi K and Kortelainen S (2017) Taking stock of empirical research on business ecosystems: A literature review. *International Journal of Business and Systems Research*, 11(3): 215–28.

6   Lucas R (1988) On the mechanics of economic development. *Journal of Monetary Economics*, 22(1): 3–42; Romer P (1990) Endogenous technological change. *Journal of Political Economy*, 98(5): S71–S102; Romer P (1994) The origins of endogenous growth. *Journal of Economic Perspectives*, 8(1): 3–22.

7   Lundvall B and Johnson B (1994) The learning economy. *Journal of Industry Studies*, 1(2): 23–42.

8   Storper M (1995) The resurgence of regional economies, ten years later: The region as a nexus of untraded interdependencies. *European Urban and Regional Studies*, 2(3): 191–221; Morgan K (1997) The learning region: institutions, innovation and regional renewal. *Regional Studies*, 31(5): 491–503.

9   Etzkowitz H and Leydesdorff L (2000) The dynamics of innovation: From National Systems and 'Mode 2' to a triple helix of university–industry–government relations. *Research Policy*, 29(2): 109–123.

10 Etzkowitz and Leydesdorff (2000), see Reference 9.

11 Beer A (2018) The closure of the Australian car manufacturing industry: Redundancy, policy and community impacts. *Australian Geographer*, 49(3): 419–438; Beer A and Thomas H (2007) The politics and policy of economic restructuring in Australia: Understanding government responses to the closure of an automotive plant. *Space and Polity*, 11(3): 243–262.

12 Bradford N (2005) *Place-Based Public Policy: Towards a New Urban and Community Agenda for Canada*. Research Report No. F|51. Ottawa: Family Network, Canadian Policy Research Networks, p. vi.

13 Barber B (2013) *If Mayors Ruled the World: Dysfunctional Nations, Rising Cities*. New Haven and London: Yale University Press.

14 Peters B and Pierre J (2004) Multi-level government – A Faustian bargain? In I Bache and M Flinders (eds.), *Multi-Level Governance*, pp. 75–89. Oxford: Oxford University Press.

15 Hambleton R (2015) Practice papers place-based leadership: A new perspective on urban regeneration. *Journal of Urban Regeneration and Renewal*, 9(1): 10–24.

16 Giddens A (2015) *Studies in Social and Political Theory*. Routledge.

17 Beal V and Pinson G (2014) When mayors go global: International strategies, urban governance and leadership. *International Journal of Urban and Regional Research*, 38(1): 302–317.

18 Tomaney J (2017) Region and place III. *Progress in Human Geography*, 41(1): 99–107, at 100.

19 Organisation for Economic Co-operation and Development (OECD) (2014) *How's Life in Your Region? Measuring Regional and Local Well-Being for Policy Making*. Paris: OECD.

20 Tomaney (2017), p. 100, see Reference 18.

21 Beer A and Evans H (2009) *The Impacts of Automotive Plant Closure: A Tale of Two Cities*. Regional Studies Association and Routledge.

22 Rainnie A, Beer A and Rafferty M (2018) *Effectiveness of Place-Based Packages: Preliminary Framework Report*. Canberra: Regional Australia Institute.

23 Editorial Committee (2014) A just transition for all: Can the past inform the future? *International Journal of Labour Research*, 6(2): 173–185, at 175.

24 Editorial Committee (2014), p. 175, see Reference 23.

25 Snell D (2018) 'Just Transition'? Conceptual challenges meet stark reality in a 'transitioning' coal region in Australia. *Globalization*, 15(4): 550–564.

26 Snell (2018), p. 550, see Reference 25.

27 Snell (2018), p. 550, see Reference 25.

28 Productivity Commission (2017) *Transitioning Regional Economies*. Study Report. Canberra: Productivity Commission, p. 29.

29 Beer A (2015) Structural adjustment programs and regional development in Australia. *Local Economy*, 30(1): 21–40.

30 Bentley G, Pugalis L and Shutt J (2017) Leadership and systems of governance: The constraints on the scope for leadership of place-based development in subnational territories. *Regional Studies*, 51(2): 194–209.

31 Rodríguez-Pose A and Wilkie C (2016) *Revamping Local and Regional Development through Place-Based Strategies*. Penn Institute for Urban Research, Working Paper prepared for Reinventing Our Communities: Transforming Our Communities, Federal Reserve Bank of Philadelphia, Biennial Conference, September.

32 Rodríguez-Pose and Wilkie (2016), p. 2, see Reference 31.

33 Bessant J, Öberg Ch and Trifilova A (2014) Framing problems in radical innovation. *Industrial Marketing Management*, 43: 1284–1292.

3. REQUIREMENTS AND CHALLENGES OF PLACE-BASED POLICY

3.1 INTRODUCTION

A defining feature of place-based policy is the need for sensitivity to local conditions and opportunities, with policies, programmes and, most especially, actions tailored to the circumstances of each place. Policies and programmes need to respond to the structural opportunities, potential and constraints locally.[1] This responsiveness has also been referred to as being 'place sensitive'.[2] Place-sensitive policies are needed to enhance the opportunities of most territories, 'regardless of their level of development or economic trajectory and taking into account local context'.[3]

From a public policy perspective there is no guaranteed template or formula for successful place-based policy. However, published policy and academic research provides a degree of guidance for the successful development of place-based programmes. Table 3.1 provides examples from the literature on place-based policy, and it can be seen that there are common themes as well as some variation depending on whether the main focus is economic development[4] or social policy (Box 3.1).[5]

Table 3.1   Key features of successful place-based policy highlighted in the literature.

	Rainne et al. (2018)[a]	VCOSS (2016)	Liu (2016)	Morgan et al. (2009)
ECONOMY	Focus on value creation and the (local) capture of value	Innovation Capacity development	Setting the right goals to expand the scope of the regional economy Growing from within to support the growth of existing and emerging firms Boosting trade to increase commerce in ways that strengthens and deepens regional industry specialisations Connecting individual places to the diverse and multiple centres of economic activity	Building and deploying local capacity to manage economic change Increasing firm access to technical assistance Establishment of clearing houses or hubs to enhance innovation Engaging higher education institutions Defining and measuring regional creative assets
TIMEFRAME	Accepting the need to adopt a long time horizon	Long-term time frames		
PEOPLE	Acknowledgement of the emotional element of change Facilitating assistance for affected individuals Targeting of assistance	Effective engagement and communication Support for groups facing disadvantage Flexible service delivery Outcomes-focused measurement Backbone funding and support Roles for community and service users	Investment in people – furthering the skills of workers must be a priority for economic development	

Sources: [a]Rainne et al. (2018), see Reference 4; VCOSS (2016), see Reference 5; Liu (2016), see Reference 4; and Morgan et al. (2009), see Reference 4.

Regional Studies Policy Impact Books

https://doi.org/10.1080/2578711X.2020.1783899
© 2020 Andrew Beer, Fiona McKenzie, Jiří Blažek,
Markku Sotarauta and Sarah Ayres

> **Box 3.1 Testing the key features of successful place-based development**
>
> Rainnie et al. (2018) (see Reference 4) developed a list of seven key features of successful place-based transitions. These transitions were largely economic in focus, reflecting the background of the researchers and the focus of the research.
>
> Seven key characteristics were tested and refined over the course of this Expo, in particular the curated discussion between academics at the Regional Studies Association (RSA) London Winter Conference workshop and policy-makers in Brussels.
>
> The lessons are summarised below:
>
> 1. Place-based policies have, by definition, a focus on place.
> 2. An engagement with local institutions is a core feature of place-based policy.
> 3. Place-based policies have a focus on governance and leadership.
> 4. Place-based policies have a focus on value creation and the local capture of value.
> 5. Place-based programmes acknowledge the need to consider the performance of places over a long time frame.
> 6. Place-based policies are a tool for targeting assistance to those individuals and groups for whom adjustment processes are most challenging.
> 7. Effective policies for addressing community disadvantage accept that there is an emotional dimension to structural change.
>
> These features had resonance with both academics and policy-makers in the team's discussions in London and Brussels. The seven features are in many ways interlinked. For example, successful engagement with local institutions (lesson 2) requires effective governance (lesson 3) and will be enhanced by leadership among local and central agencies as well as by government and non-government actors. Leadership is also a theme that connects the social and emotional aspects of structural change (lesson 7) among those most affected by that change (lesson 6) in order to maximise future value creation (lesson 4).

Because of this interconnectedness, the remainder of this chapter considers the requirements for successful place-based policy in a holistic way, based on the following premise: successful place-based policy requires institutional capacity, which consists of good quality governance and leadership.

3.2 GOVERNANCE

In practical terms, governance is characterised by both planned as well as unplanned interactions amongst various stakeholders across organisational boundaries, and these enable the exchange of resources and the alignment of competences and interests. Governance can be defined as decision-making arrangements that consist of both formal and informal structures of power and administration that have the capacity to alter existing institutions or to create new ones.[6] Governance acknowledges the multi-actor and multi-scalar (i.e., operating locally, regionally and nationally) nature of contemporary regional development and underlines the need to build formal and informal collaborative structures that encourage mutual understanding and learning. Governance arrangements can be used to encourage various forms of innovation: economic, social or environmental.[7]

Recent political and academic discourse about place-based policy has stressed the importance of strong and competent local governance arrangements; indeed, the quality of regional and local government can be a direct determinant of local economic growth and productivity. Cities with many local governments tend to have lower levels of productivity such that, for a given population size, a metropolitan area with twice the number of municipalities is associated with around 6% lower productivity.[8] Importantly, this effect is reduced by half by the presence of a governance body at the metropolitan level. Enhancing the capacity of subnational governments to achieve their political and economic objectives in collaboration with partners provides a dynamic tool with which to help municipal governments shape local policy.[9] Small local governments do not always have the power to influence others working at multiple levels. More specifically, having local control over resources – fiscal decentralisation – is an important feature of empowered local institutions and their ability to enact place-based initiatives. The economic growth effects of decentralisation depend on the fiscal authority of subnational governments.[10]

There is a strong consensus that civic participation is a necessary feature of successful place-based initiatives. This is found in work by policy-makers[11] as well as academics.[12] *A focus on governance means local individuals and businesses gain access to decision-making*. These groups are deemed expert by their lived experience and enduring interest in the well-being of the community or region. They may also form the nucleus of community-led regeneration partnerships. These new institutional arrangements enable those designing and implementing place-based policies to strengthen the relationship between governments and citizens.

Smart Specialisation is an example of place-based policy characterised as a root-and-branch transformation of the governance of regional policy (Figure 3.1):

> *it is aimed at transforming policy thinking from top-down and predominantly sectorally-led approaches to a more local, bottom-up approach. Such bottom-up approaches may include the enhancing of local skills and training, accelerating the transfer and adoption of new technologies, creating incubators and/or the implementation of cluster policy implementation … it emphasises the local policy prioritisation process, where policy interventions … are identified through local stakeholders.[13]*

Good governance is not always easy to achieve, and there are challenges at both the local level and at higher levels of government. European governance initiatives aiming to redress uneven spatial development have often placed communities at their core. This body of experimentation and evaluation has shown that the empowerment of communities is a necessary, but not sufficient, step towards transition at the local level. Programmes and policies that focus solely on local communities taking control of their destiny, but which failed to provide funding or other supports, were unable to meet either their narrowly defined goals, or the broader expectations of society.

Figure 3.1   Smart Specialisation: strengthening local industries

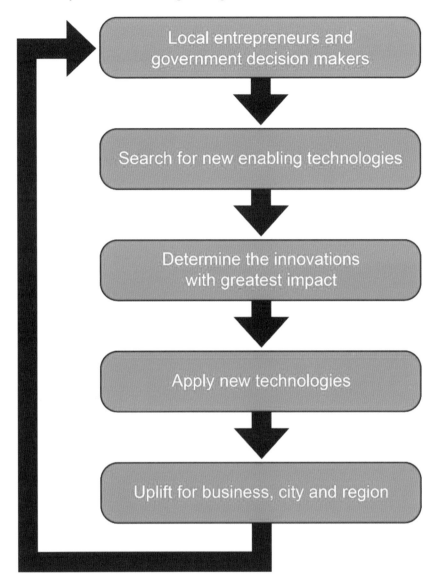

Regional and local governance is often hamstrung by the continued dominance of the political and administrative centre and tensions between multilevel governance tiers.[14] Delivering place-based policy is particularly challenging where there is a high degree of central government control.

In their analysis of 39 European countries between 1990 and 2014, Ladner et al.[15] showed that local autonomy is a highly valued feature of good local governance. They argued that while there has been an overall increase in local autonomy across Europe, there is significant variation between countries that can undermine policy development and democratic renewal efforts. For example, English devolution is characterised by a strong degree of central government control that has created tensions between governance tiers and a public mistrust and apathy towards place-based initiatives.[16] Place-based policy often conceals power struggles and tensions that can undermine policy effectiveness, especially when there is an inescapable 'shadow of hierarchy'.

The link between place-based policy and enhanced democracy is not automatic and much will depend on how territories manage their governance structures and engender a spirit of inclusiveness. Local governments may, for example, find it difficult to respond adequately to the needs and aspirations of citizens. Indeed, public apathy and mistrust is often cited as a barrier to the success of place-based initiatives. In their analysis of 27 member states of the European Union plus Norway and Switzerland, Loughlin et al.[17] analysed the quality of local democracy. They focused on the practice of democracy, including the roles of political parties and interest groups and also how local political institutions related to ordinary citizen. Their research revealed a wide variety of practices. Among the challenges identified were citizens' disaffection and 'switch-off' from politics.

Some countries have confronted these challenges more successfully than others, but all countries face them. For example, Lackowska and Mikula[18] drew on a case study of Poland where city-region governance was both developed and effective, but where public support remained low. Their findings showed that *even when local institutions were effective, there remained barriers to the public engaging with an administrative tier to which they had little affiliation. This underscores the argument made earlier about the importance of local identity as a route to successful place-based policy-making.*

3.2.1 The governance of Smart Specialisation

While the need for sound governance in the implementation of Smart Specialisation is acknowledged, practical challenges remain. Regions are diverse with respect to their economic structure as well as their cultural, institutional and organisational assets. This challenges the feasibility of a one-size-fits-all policy.[19] Inevitably, therefore, a wide spectrum of governance systems has arisen across regions, reflecting nation-specific features such as the general level of centralisation or decentralisation within the system of public administration. Prominent among these is the role of path dependency as few, if any, developed regions started their Smart Specialisation strategy from a blank canvas.

Consequently, the first dilemma when contemplating suitable Smart Specialisation governance is whether (or to what extent) existing governance structures for innovation policy are able to deliver this new programme of action. Is it the case that processes such as the entrepreneurial-discovery process generate new requirements and actions that are better delivered via new structures?

Similarly, there is a question as to whether to rely (or, again, to what extent to rely) upon the engagement of established and respected stakeholders, or if it would be better to call on voices that emerged more recently? The latter are more likely to reflect the experience of new and innovative firms in the region. Importantly, when selecting suitable stakeholders, the envisaged and actual functions fulfilled by these stakeholders should be articulated carefully.[20] Individual capacities are highly differentiated, and the ability of any one individual to contribute productively may be dependent upon electoral cycles or the potentially variable commitment of large public entities such as universities. The rotation of senior management in large corporations may also play a role, as will personal characteristics, such as the willingness of individuals to both lead and follow, as well as to cooperate with others.

The third dilemma in governance for Smart Specialisation concerns the stability of governance structures. Namely, how do governments ensure that the governance system they create is open to new personalities and new ideas, while safeguarding the coherence of the whole? On the one hand, governance structures have to be sufficiently stable to operate across an enduring time span to function effectively and have individuals become productive in their roles. On the other, an ever-changing reality (both within and outside of the region) may require substantial flexibility and adaptability. It takes a substantial period for new members of various governance structures to recognise the expectations upon them and what they, in turn, can expect of others. Only after a sustained period can individuals offer a real contribution.

Finally, a highly sensitive dilemma for Smart Specialisation concerns the inclusiveness of the governance structure. The openness of the system to a broad spectrum of stakeholders (such as those interested in innovative public tendering, social innovation, innovations in health care, etc.) is valuable in its own right. However, such broad participation may limit the interest of key stakeholders as some themes lie outside their interests and, consequently, they will either not join or quickly exit governance arrangements. More importantly, such broad conceptions of participation in governance raise unrealistic expectations, which undermines the credibility of the system as a whole.

The dilemmas outlined above need not be seen as insurmountable barriers to place-based development. Rather, they can be used to structure the thinking of key stakeholders as they map out governance structures. While Smart Specialisation governance structures already exist in all European Union countries and many regions, the evolutionary dynamics of modern economies imply a need to reconsider the function and design of existing governance. It is useful to recall that one of the key propositions of the new industrial development model is the argument that the new path starts when the new institutional structure established to support this new trajectory (Box 3.2).[21]

Box 3.2   Sound governance structures

Despite the impossibility of providing universal recipes, the following features of a sound governance structure for Smart Specialisation or other place-based policies should be highlighted:

- Governance structures should be strongly backed by political representation and the need to encompass relevant actors from public administration, private companies and academia.
- The system of governance should be sufficiently stable to accommodate change as needed. Some regions use a system where the Smart Specialisation steering committee represents a stable 'core', while various working groups are established in the short term and some are project based.

- Governance structures should be supported by a professional and highly committed organisation(s) with a clear vision devoted to support the development of the region. This organisation should be endowed with sufficient resources (human, material), but also be able to mobilise substantial social capital from both within and outside the region by being constantly 'in the field', that is, in close contact with various stakeholders. There is a need to investigate new initiatives through networking, forming coalitions around entrepreneurial individuals and organisations. It can take a decade to build solid social capital. Trust, negotiation and collaboration skills are indispensable.
- Governance structures should be properly aligned to Smart Specialisation priorities, while fully acknowledging that the form of alignment varies from region to region.

3.3 LEADERSHIP

Leadership is an overarching precondition for effective place-based policy. It connects the many aspects that were outlined above in section 1. For example, the subjective experience of change, which may include emotion and individual well-being, is not separate from the policy-making process. People have a very strong sense of place which is important in their material and subjective world. Peoples' attitudes and behaviours are shaped by their perception of place.

As change is implemented, governments need to address two separate, but interrelated, phenomena. First, they need to consciously acknowledge peoples' sense of connection to place. This can be done by branding their programmes and emphasising the priority given to the localities in which people live. Second, they need to address the channels through which these messages are delivered, using local leaders as trusted sources of information and opinion formation. This approach creates an important conduit for achieving the 'buy-in' of residents, a sense of the value and legitimacy of the place-based policy being rolled out, and a perception of the worth being bestowed on the community through this policy. This process of trust-building can enable the emotional aspects of change to be acknowledged by government.

Local leadership can be a route to policy effectiveness. Directly-elected mayors, for example, provide visible and publicly accountable local leadership with the potential to provide a dynamic, adaptive and facilitative role in the pursuit of local policies. However, not all key actors shaping the future of regions and cities are necessarily appointed through elections. Non-governmental leaders also have a pivotal role in promoting public participation and engagement in policy-making.[22]

Leadership is fundamental to successful place-based policies because of its importance in building collective agency and local capacity. It can assist in aligning institutional settings to the specificities of a particular place. This collective agency connects three things: public administration, everyday local practices and knowledge. This potential for productive interaction may be given life by a process of experimentation – in terms of possible futures, ways of mobilising resources, the sharing of knowledge and managing relations with others – that is iterative and allows solutions to emerge over time. These 'operational interfaces', it has been argued, are key to the successful implementation of place-based approaches.

Ideally, place-based policy is an inclusive and bottom-up process that looks to the actors and assets embedded in each locality to find answers to the major challenges of policy-making and implementation. These challenges include: how to identify regional assets; how to mobilise a wide spectrum of actors in a policy design and implementation; and how to set priorities for action from amongst competing claims for action and in the face of numerous local voices.[23] For these reasons, just as leadership is critical to place-based policy, the absence of leadership can undermine attempts to formulate and implement such policy.

Governments often struggle to meet the needs of specific places because of competing interests and the failure of the wider public to understand the complex challenges confronting localities. There may also be a tendency of some central government agencies to seek to retain control. *But commonly one of the greatest challenges faced by governments, elected officials and professional officers alike is the difficulty in implementing long-term solutions.* A potential answer to these challenges may lie in the power of local leadership in cities, regions and small communities. *As place leaders*, they have a commitment and vested interest in enhancing the well-being of the places in which they live. They have specific knowledge of the local area and provide social networks and other resources that assist the delivery of policies. Importantly, they *have the capacity and motivation to take a long-term perspective* (Figure 3.2).

Figure 3.2   **Local leaders and place-based policy**

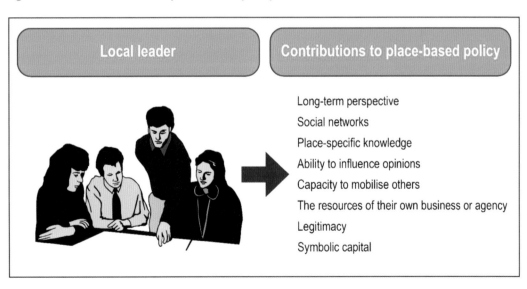

Place leadership looks beyond formal policies to draw on the resources of individuals and groups to bring about the betterment of that community. It may, or may not, have a relationship with the formal structures of authority – government departments or committees – and it seeks to achieve change through persuasion, influence and the mobilisation of social dynamics.[24] Place-based leadership is not synonymous with the local leadership discussed in the above section: good local leadership is critical in providing a public face to place-based policy efforts, one that is attached to the formal powers of government in some way, and able to serve as a conduit for central government and public attention. Place-based leadership, by contrast, is not necessarily public-facing, and often draws its strength from networks and processes that attract little public attention.

A focus on place leadership and its contribution to place-based policy guides us to ask questions about how diverse groups of actors are encouraged to work towards a common purpose, how their actions can be coordinated for the collective good. By definition, place-leadership works across institutional, organisational, geographical and/or sectoral boundaries to amplify the local power base and strengthen its capacity to influence the development of a place.[25]

Place-based policy may provide place leaders with a platform they can influence, or place leadership may take place outside the formal policy sphere to achieve its own ends. Alternatively, place leadership may work through sectoral policies as well as regional policy to draw and pool resources for the betterment of that locality. In all instances, the concept of place leadership directs our attention to actors influencing place-based policy design and implementation, and the ways individuals influence events regardless of a policy apparatus:

There seems to be a growing understanding of the question not only being about the need to co-design 'better' policies, to ensure much wider participation and inclusion in policy process and the continuing integration of governance, but very much also about the most appropriate ways of leading in and across all this activity.[26]

Critically, place-based leadership creates both challenges and opportunities for policy-makers and the implementation of their policy designs. On the one hand, place leaders represent a resource for central governments, able to bring together social connections and information that is enabling of governmental programmes and able to magnify their impact. On the other, *places that lack such leadership may be further disadvantaged – making it harder to help places already confronting difficult circumstances.* Local elites may also entrench vested interests[27] – giving priority to their own interests and locking the economy into a pathway of decline as they provide support to established businesses and prevent the emergence of new sectors and business models.

In the research teams' discussions with policy-makers and regional researchers, two very different perceptions of the role of leadership in place-based policy emerged:

- Researchers felt place-based leadership was central to the realisation of place-based policy ambitions, serving to bring those goals to life while also fine-tuning strategies and objectives, building local support, and cutting across bureaucratic boundaries.

- By contrast, policy-makers were unaware of the role leaders play in target communities, instead focusing on the importance of governance and governmental structures.

This gap in the perceptions of two key groups in the policy-formation process raises questions for the further development of this area of public policy.

3.4 POLICY CHALLENGES

3.4.1 Faltering expectations

Success in public policy is a struggle at a societal and governmental level, often over who gets what, and why. Indeed, any public policy process involves a complex set of elements which are difficult to identify and interpret. Moreover, correctly interpreting which factors directly influence local growth and which play a lesser role represents a significant challenge that may not be assisted by a local perspective.

In many countries it has become habitual to talk about challenges instead of problems, to focus more on strengths and opportunities than weaknesses and threats. For their part, place-based policy processes need positive future-oriented attitudes and approaches to taking action. Additionally, place-based policy calls for thorough analysis of institutional failings that undermine the implementation of even the best policy designs. Identification of, and systematic work to eliminate, fundamental weaknesses should be part of the standard repertoire of policy analysis. Many well-known, and often reported, issues include vested interests, institutional conflicts, corruption, lack of capabilities to manage complex processes, fragmented funding and measurement bias.

The importance of robust but flexible institutional arrangements, good governance and dynamic place leadership is necessary for successful place-based policy, but does not guarantee success. Place-based policies may get bogged down in a vicious circle of faltering expectations and piecemeal solutions (Figure 3.3) if not able to realise their ambitions. Devising a solution to an identified challenge without appropriate efforts to strengthen governance capacity or develop new capabilities – a more skilled workforce, leading-edge technologies or infrastructure, a more supportive business environment – is likely to lead to failed policy or the partial implementation of grand ideas. This potentially leads to disappointment and the subsequent need to reframe the original problem, underscoring the challenge, but with a new vocabulary. At its worst, this leads to an endless circle where new buzz words and fashionable models replace analytical thinking and thus opportunities are not seized and weaknesses not eliminated.

Figure 3.3   A vicious circle of faltering expectations

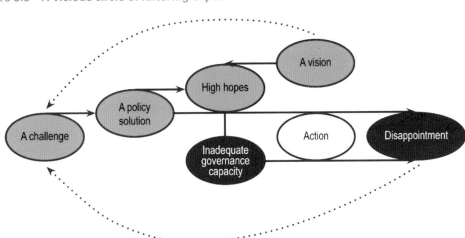

The underlying assumptions – the ideal – of place-based policy are to be welcomed warmly, but extra care should be given to turning the vicious circle of faltering expectations into a positive and self-reinforcing circle of fulfilled aspirations. Disappointments need to be transformed into a positive feedback loop of a sequence of achievements, the development of locally rooted skills and policy capabilities, and the expansion of place-based leadership.

3.4.2 Vested interests

Policy-making often involves many different actors including: government officials, elected members, legislators, interest groups, the media and others. Each actor may have different values, perceptions and interests. A complicating factor in the policy process is that most disputes involve deeply held values/interests, substantial money and, at some point, authoritative coercion. Given these stakes, policy disputes seldom resemble polite academic debates. Instead, most actors face enormous temptation to present evidence selectively, to misrepresent the position of their opponents, to coerce and discredit opponents, and generally to distort the situation to their advantage.

Vested interests represent a challenge for the development and implementation of place-based policy, but it is a challenge matched by shifts in wider political agendas and priorities. These shifting priorities may reflect both party political change – as one group of elected officials replaces another in government – but also the varying priorities of key professional decision-makers. Policy-makers in Brussels, for example, noted shifts in the degree of attention paid to place-based policies over the past two decades. There was a perception that while the recommendations of the Barca Review[28] were accepted and formally adopted, less was achieved than needed in order to deliver the forecast outcomes.

More recently the European Union has given a greater emphasis to place-centred approaches. Focus group participants who worked in European local governments noted the hurdles they faced attempting to accommodate local conditions, priorities and needs within the programmes offered by national governments and the European Union. Overall, the challenges of delivering place-sensitive approaches, at scale, in an ever-shifting policy and political landscape appear to be substantial.

3.4.3 Lack of financial resources

A key barrier to the effective provision of local policy-making and public services is the absence or shortage of financial resources. This issue has been particularly acute since the global financial crisis in 2008. A key challenge for place-based policy is when nation-states seek to decentralise responsibility, but not the necessary resources required for implementation. For example, Del Pino and Pavolini[29] explored how austerity has affected the decentralised management of public services in Spain and Italy. To receive support or extra funding, regional governments accepted the conditions imposed by central government. Their findings indicate that central control, austerity and public sector cuts can threaten decentralised budgets and undermine the discretion of locally based public service solutions.

Lowndes and Gardner[30] argue that places face substantial obstacles in attempting to engage communities in an era of financial crisis and austerity. Based on their analysis of decentralisation in the UK, they contend that local governments confront 'super-austerity', where new cuts to public sector spending come on top of previous expressions of austerity, compounding the original impacts and creating dangerous (and unevenly spread) multiplier effects that undermine local development and damage public service provision.

Cuts to public services can lead to enhanced competition between communities, which has the potential to create an introverted, and sometimes exclusionary, political community. Subsequent attempts to redress local political divisions can divert energy and resources away from the more routine, but no less important, task of providing efficient services. Nevertheless, it has to be emphasised that place-based policies are not necessarily about performing new spending activities more effectively, but can also offer a more efficient way of delivering existing policies and programmes. Thus, place-based policies can represent one tool to overcome funding limitations.

3.4.4 Measuring success

While the previous chapters have indicated a broad level of agreement about the benefits of, and require ments for, successful place-based development, there is less consensus on whether place-based policies have been a success. One reason for this difficulty is a conceptual one. Too often in discussions about place-based policy, researchers, government officials and commentators alike assume that the nature, intent and implementation of place-based policy is self-evident. However, there is considerable variation in how place-based policy is conceived and it is an area of public sector activity that embraces a wide variety of policy domains. Because of their potential complexity, place-based policies must be developed with very clear objectives and scope. There is a need for adequate benchmarking and measurement so that policy initiatives can be assessed against intended outcomes. Such monitoring of performance can only be achieved if the goals of the project or policies are clear – an ill-defined concept is unlikely to be easily measured or measured at all.

Performance monitoring of spatial governance arrangements is generally underused in the delivery of public services.[31] Closer attention to standard benchmarks and performance monitoring could help to ascertain the effectiveness of place-based policies. Furthermore, the development of such measures at the start of a programme can force policy-makers to develop an outcomes orientation from inception; to bring realism in the project's design; and to provide a basis for assessing whether the programme is having its intended impacts.[32]

The principles underlying place-based policy, such as local focus and civic participation, also highlight the importance *of qualitative as well as quantitative outcome measures*, particularly in relation to measures of well-being. Measurement of such attributes in local and regional terms connects policy-makers to debates about the importance of place attachments in the formation of socioeconomic, political and ethical values.[33] In analysing the issues facing regional policy in Wales, Brill et al.[34] suggested regions need to develop new metrics and a multi-indicator economic and social 'dashboard' in order assess improvements in population welfare. They suggested this would ensure a much clearer focus on deficiencies in the provision of what they term 'foundational' goods and services for all the population (housing, transport and utility supply, health, education, care, and food).

Indeed, monitoring the performance of place-based policy is a daunting task; there are many intervening forces such that the relationship between a policy intention and outcomes is far from linear. Ideally governments in partnership with the community would develop metrics, quantitative and qualitative, which operate at three levels:

- Short-term results — the relationship between the policy and the direct outcomes: Did the projects implementing policy meet their short-term goals? Did the projects, investments and other policy measures form a coherent entity?

- Long term impacts — the relationship between the policy intention and issues that gave rise to government action. Did the policy nudge development into the desired direction?

- Significance for the development work — the relationship between policy intentions and how programmes were implemented. Were new skills learnt and competencies developed? Were new networks internal and external to the region established? Did place leadership develop? Significance refers to all those factors that improve the institutional arrangements and governance capacity.

This kind of framework was used in an evaluation of regional development policy in the Northern Tampere Region of Finland. The results revealed that almost all the policy measures met their short-term goals, but their impact on regional development was minimal. On the other hand, the significance of the development work resulted in new networks internal and external to the region, new development capabilities, and a more comprehensive approach to local development.[35]

3.5 CONCLUSIONS

This chapter has examined the governmental processes that underpin and shape place-based policies in order to identify the factors that are likely to lead to the success or failure of such programmes. The review of the published literature and discussions with policy-makers and researchers has highlighted two critical preconditions for success in place-based policy:

- *Good governance arrangements are essential if place-based policies and programmes are to achieve their goals.* This means that the arrangements that provide an oversight of such initiatives must include an appropriate mix of stakeholders, including those representative of disadvantaged groups as well as those with the power to bring about change through the organisations they lead or work within, and the resources they contribute to this shared objective. Good governance calls for well-understood aims, but also transparent and robust processes around information-sharing and decision-making. As noted in this chapter, individuals and groups within affected communities need to have a share of decision-making power, and such arrangements are essential if there is to be a local 'buy-in'.

- *Local leaders need to be an integral component of all place-based policy designs and implementation.* Their active involvement is essential in order to achieve the mobilisation of community resources, a long-term perspective and the patience to work towards goals in the distant future, and community acknowledgement of the value of such policies.

In our work on this Policy Expo we drew on the work of Rainnie et al.[36] and argued that place-based policies:

- have, by definition, a focus on place;

- involve engagement with local institutions as a core feature;

- have a focus on governance;

- emphasise value creation and the local capture of value;

- acknowledge the need to consider the performance of places over a long time frame;

- are an important tool for targeting assistance to those individuals and groups for whom adjustment processes are most challenging; and

- accept that there is an emotional dimension to structural change.

These propositions were accepted by policy-makers at the Brussels workshop and researchers in London alike, and we would add three additional insights to our understanding of success in place-based policy:

- It is important to set up outcome and output measures – qualitative and quantitative – early in the implementation of place-based initiatives in order to drive achievement.

- Faltering expectations and a cycle of disillusionment should be avoided by having demonstrable, significant, achievements built into the programme design, which can be short term, long term or developmental, and they need to be communicated to all stakeholders, including the wider community.

- There needs to be a clear focus on the goals and aspirations of the place-based policy at inception, and these need to be agreed to by all stakeholders.

REFERENCES

1 Rodríguez-Pose A (2018) The revenge of the places that don't matter (and what to do about it). *Cambridge Journal of Regions, Economy and Society*, 11(1): 189–209.

2 Iammarino S, Rodríguez-Pose A and Storper M (2017) *Why Regional Development Matters for Europe's Economic Future*. Working Papers of the Directorate-General for Regional and Urban Policy WP 07/2017. Brussels: European Commission.

3 Rodríguez-Pose A (2018), p. 205, see Reference 1.

4 Morgan J, Lambe W and Freyer A (2009) Homegrown responses to economic uncertainty in rural America. *Rural Realities*, 3(2): 1–14; Liu A (2016) *Remaking Economic Development – The Markets and Civics of Continuous Growth and*

Prosperity. Metropolitan Policy Program. Washington, DC: The Brookings Institution; Rainnie A, Beer A and Rafferty M (2018) *Effectiveness of Place-Based Packages: Preliminary Framework Report.* Canberra: Regional Australia Institute.

5   Victorian Council of Social Service (VCOSS) (2016) *Unleashing the Power of Communities: A Social Innovation Fund for Place-Based Policy.* Melbourne: VCOSS. Available online at: https://www.vcoss.org.au/analysis/unleashing-the-power-of-communities-a-social-innovation-fund-for-place-based-initiatives/

6   Sotarauta M and Beer A (2017) Governance, agency and place leadership: Lessons from a cross-national analysis. *Regional Studies,* 51(2): 210–223.

7   Hassink R and Gong H (2019) Six critical questions about Smart Specialisation. *European Planning Studies,* 7(10): 2049–2065.

8   Ahrend R, Farchy E, Kaplanis I and Lembcke A (2014) *What Makes Cities More Productive? Evidence on the Role of Urban Governance from Five OECD Countries.* Regional Development Working Papers. Paris: Organisation for Economic Co-operation and Development (OECD).

9   Eckersley P (2017) A new framework for understanding subnational policy-making and local choice. *Policy Studies,* 38(1): 76–90.

10 Filippetti A and Cerulli G (2018) Are local public services better delivered in more autonomous regions? Evidence from European regions using a dose-response approach. *Papers in Regional Science,* 97(3): 801–826.

11 Organisation for Economic Co-operation and Development (OECD) (2009) *Regions Matter: Economic Recovery, Innovation and Sustainable Growth.* Paris: OECD; OECD (2012) *Promoting Growth in All Regions.* Paris: OECD.

12 Horlings L, Roep D and Wellbrock W (2018) The role of leadership in place-based development and building institutional arrangements. *Local Economy,* 33(3): 245–268; Bentley G, Pugalis L and Shutt J (2017) Leadership and systems of governance: The constraints on the scope for leadership of place-based development in subnational territories. *Regional Studies,* 51(2): 194–209.

13 McCann P and Ortega-Argilés R (2019) Perspectives on Smart Specialisation policies in lagging regions. In M Barzotto, C Corrandini, M Fai, S Labory and P Tomlinson (eds.), *Revitalising Lagging Regions: Smart Specialisation and Industry 4.0,* pp. 17–29, at 19. Abingdon: Taylor & Francis.

14 Ayres S and Stafford I (2014) Managing complexity and uncertainty in regional governance networks: A critical analysis of state rescaling in England. *Regional Studies,* 48(1): 219–235.

15 Ladner A, Keuffer N and Baldersheim H (2016) Measuring local autonomy in 39 countries (1990–2014). *Regional and Federal Studies,* 26(3): 321–357. doi:10.1080/13597566.2016.1214911

16 Ayres S, Sandford M and Coombes T (2017) Policy-making 'front' and 'back' stage: Assessing the implications for effectiveness and democracy. *British Journal of Politics and International Relations,* 19(4): 861–876.

17 Loughlin J, Henriks F and Lidstrom A (2012) *Oxford Handbook of Local and Regional Democracy in Europe.* Oxford: Oxford University Press.

18 Lackowska M and Mikula L (2015) How metropolitan can you go? Citizenship in Polish city-regions. *Journal of Urban Affairs,* 35(1): 12–36.

19 Tödtling F and Trippl M (2005) One size fits all? Towards a differentiated regional innovation policy approach. *Research Policy,* 34(8): 1203–1219.

20 Uyarra E and Flanagan K (2010) From regional systems of innovations to regions as innovation policy spaces. *Environment and Planning C: Government and Policy,* 28(4): 681–695. doi:10.1068/c0961

21 Hassink R, Isaksen A and Trippl M (2019) Towards a comprehensive understanding of new regional industrial path development. *Regional Studies*, 53(11): 1636–1645; Sotarauta M and Mustikkamäki N (2015) Institutional entrepreneurship, power, and knowledge in innovation systems: Institutionalization of regenerative medicine in Tampere, Finland. *Environment and Planning C: Government and Policy*, 33(2): 342–357.

22 Ayres S (2019) How can network leaders promote public value through soft metagovernance? *Public Administration*, 97(2): 279–295.

23 Sotarauta M (2018) Smart Specialization and place leadership: Dreaming about shared visions, falling into policy traps? *Regional Studies, Regional Science*, 5(1): 190–203.

24 Sotarauta M (2016) *Leadership and the City: Power, Strategy and Networks in the Making of Knowledge Cities.* Abingdon: Routledge.

25 Blažek J, Žížalová P, Rumpel P, Skokan K and Chládek P (2013) Emerging regional innovation strategies in Central Europe: Institutions and regional leadership in generating strategic outcomes. *European Urban and Regional Studies*, 20(2): 275–294.

26 Sotarauta M, Beer A and Gibney J (2017) Making sense of leadership in urban and regional development. *Regional Studies*, 51(2): 187–193, at 190.

27 Sabatier P (2007) The need for better theories. In P Sabatier (ed.), *Theories of the Policy Process*, pp. 3–17. Boulder, Colorado: Westview Press.

28 Barca F (2009) *An Agenda for a Reformed Cohesion Policy.* Independent report to the Commissioner for Regional Policy. Brussels: European Union.

29 Del Pino E and Pavolini E (2015) Decentralisation at a time of harsh austerity: Multilevel governance and the welfare state in Spain and Italy facing the crisis. *European Journal of Social Security*, 17(2): 246–270.

30 Lowndes V and Gardner A (2016) Local governance under the Conservatives: Super-austerity, devolution and the 'smarter state'. *Local Government Studies*, 42(3): 357–375.

31 Lewis C and Fall F (2017) *Enhancing Public Sector Efficiency and Effectiveness in the Czech Republic.* Working Paper. Paris: Organisation for Economic Co-operation and Development (OECD).

32 McCann P (2019) *UK Research and Innovation: A Place-Based Shift?* UK Research and Innovation, p. 14.

33 Tomaney J (2014) Region and place I: Institutions. *Progress in Human Geography*, 38(1): 131–140. doi:10.1177/0309132513493385

34 Brill L, Cowie L, Folkman A, Froud J, Johal S, Leaver A, Moran M and Williams K (2015) *What Wales Could Be.* Report for FSB Wales. Manchester: Centre for Research on Socio-Cultural Change (CRESC).

35 Viljamaa K (2000) *Suuria odotuksia, pieniä askelia. Pohjois-Pirkanmaan strategisen ohjelmatyön 1995–1999 arviointi* [Evaluation of the Strategic Development Program in Northern Tampere Region 1995–1999]. Sente Publications No. 8/2000: Tampere: University of Tampere, Research Unit for Urban and Regional Development Studies.

36 Rainnie et al. (2018), see Reference 4.

4. OUTCOMES OF PLACE-BASED POLICY: WHAT WORKS AND WHAT DOES NOT?

4.1 INTRODUCTION

The previous chapters have highlighted the benefits, features and challenges of place-based policies. This chapter uses several case studies to show how these elements have played out in real-world examples. In so doing, it aims to provide readers, both academic and policy related, with insights into what approaches have worked or not, and under what circumstances this has occurred. By the very nature of place-based policy, it will not answer every question for every locality. However, there is value in documenting the lessons already learnt.

An understanding of the philosophy and strategic intent of place-based approaches is important, but it is critical also to understand also how such initiatives are positioned with respect to each locality and what they aspire to achieve. It is important for policy-makers to have a strong appreciation of what the evidence base indicates is, and is not, in scope with respect to place-based policy. Fortunately, there is now a considerable body of published work that reflects experience with place-based programmes and provides the insights needed to inform decision-making. This chapter draws on insights from around the globe to ground the discussion in real-world examples.

4.2 PLACE-BASED POLICIES IN RESPONSE TO AN ECONOMIC SHOCK: THE LATROBE VALLEY IN GIPPSLAND, AUSTRALIA

As discussed in chapter 2, section 5, the Latrobe Valley in the Gippsland region of southern Australia has been the subject of government policy to address issues of economic transition and structural adjustment. This began in the 1990s following privatisation of electricity generation, a sector upon which the Latrobe Valley was particularly dependent. More recently, following the closure of the Hazelwood coal-fired power station in 2017, a more innovative policy approach was undertaken, based on the principles of Smart Specialisation developed in the European Union.

There are three major settlements within the Latrobe Valley: Moe, Morwell and Traralgon. Effective governance in the region has traditionally been challenged by differences between these settlements and the fact that, before the 1990s, they each formed their own municipality. Amalgamation of these small municipalities into the city of Latrobe in 1994 did not automatically deliver effective governance or economic productivity gains, nor did it overcome parochial attitudes which had been embedded in the pre-existing municipal structure. A further challenge was the concurrent privatisation of the electricity sector which brought major job losses and had a profound impact on the region. The reliance on brown coal for electricity generation has continued to create economic risk as the world moves towards a low-carbon economy. Yet, relinquishing a local identity that has been entwined with the mining and energy sector has been emotionally difficult for the community.

The Latrobe Valley Authority (LVA) was established in late 2016 in response to the impending closure of Hazelwood power station in 2017. It aimed to bring together government, business, research and education,

https://doi.org/10.1080/2578711X.2020.1783900

and civil society in the Gippsland region to co-design a shared vision for the region's future prosperity, environmental sustainability and social well-being. This approach was a break from past approaches of top-down assistance packages from state and federal government. Instead, the LVA was based locally and aimed to facilitate collaboration among local stakeholders, while providing a framework for identifying and understanding the region's knowledge assets, expertise and strengths. The 'region' was expanded beyond the Latrobe Valley itself, encompassing the larger regional entity of Gippsland. This assisted in identifying new connections and opportunities beyond the industrial sectors located in the valley to a wider range of regional activities, such as horticulture, in the larger Gippsland region. The LVA has facilitated a process of broad engagement of regional stakeholders including policy-makers, business, research and education, and community, thus providing a quadruple helix approach. Importantly, it identified a staged approach to the region's needs, starting with an immediate response to issues such as the Hazelwood closure and subsequent high rates of local unemployment, followed by recovery and capability-building as the second-stage focus and then, beyond this, strategic and sustainable growth.

The approach draws explicitly on the principle of co-design with regional stakeholders with the LVA mission stated as follows:

Our Mission

To work with and for the people of Latrobe Valley to:

- Build on community strengths and capability for the future

- Lead collaboration and innovation

- Draw on and use the best ideas for what works, both locally and from outside the region

- Support opportunity for all[1]

Through an entrepreneurial discovery process, different scenarios for future development paths for the region were explored in order to develop a shared vision for the future and an agreed set of priorities. This led to the selection of several regional priorities for specialisation, each of which could provide growth and innovation, have the capacity to build critical mass and be competitive. These included: food and fibre (all of Gippsland); new energy; health and well-being; and tourism.

The horticulture sector was selected as the starting point for mapping the regional innovation ecosystem and the strengths and capabilities of the local economy and its community. One reason for this was that the sector was already looking for assistance. It approached the LVA and the project to date has developed governance around the food and fibre sector in Gippsland.

The three Latrobe Valley settlements mentioned above have received government investment over recent years including: rail transport, sports facilities, community facilities and a major 'GovHub' office in which various government functions will be located with around 200 public sector staff. The region is going through a transforming phase with improvements to the physical appearance of settlements in the region and the establishment of public amenities such as the local art gallery. In terms of education, there has been development of the local technical education campus and expansion of the regional university (Federation University). On the surface, these investments might be seen as traditional assistance from central government agencies. However, the development of Smart Specialisation processes provided an overarching framework that informed decision-making and created a positive story of change.

There have been important private sector investments through the university and health sectors aligned with the Smart Specialisation agenda. For example, the expansion of the regional health sector may simply be viewed as a reflection of an ageing population requiring more services. Yet, in the context of the Smart Specialisation framework, this expansion can be linked to opportunities for collaborative initiatives aimed at attracting a skilled workforce to the region or, indeed, to train one locally in collaboration with local tertiary institutions. Attracting specialist and skilled labour to the region continues to be a challenge, as it is in many other non-metropolitan regions of Australia. The next phase of Smart Specialisation that will be rolled out by the LVA relates to the workforce in the health sector and other industries in the area. It aims to align sectors to achieve continuous innovation and collaboration.

While parochialism still exists in the region, the city of Latrobe municipal staff now work very much as a single entity.[2] It has been important to demonstrate to the community that collaboration can generate individual benefit – the two are not mutually exclusive. At the same time, it is recognised that the community faces particular challenges. Yallourn power station (within the Latrobe municipality) has indicated it may close in the short or medium term, and this is a cause of anxiety. Although the closure of Hazelwood did not have as significant an impact as some expected, there remains a real identity associated with coal, and hence closures are taken very badly.[3] This highlights the importance of acknowledging, and being sensitive to, the emotional aspects of change when undertaking place-based initiatives.

While the Smart Specialisation approach is relatively new within the Latrobe Valley, its initial work in the face of industry closure seems to have been successful – three-quarters of former Hazelwood employees have found jobs since the closure.[4] Initiatives such as the Worker Transfer Scheme brought government, unions and employers together. Stage 2 (recovery and capability building) initiatives are connecting local training sectors with workforce needs in priority sectors such as healthcare. The connection between government and local business is enabling local suppliers to be used in public sector procurement, while the development of public sports facilities is seen within the wider context of addressing public health and well-being issues that have existed in the region for many years. Collaboration and connection at the local level appears to be a key feature of the programme of place-based development being facilitated through the LVA.

4.3 PLACE-BASED POLICIES FOR INNOVATION AND ECONOMIC GROWTH: FINLAND AND SWEDEN

Recent policy developments in Scandinavia provide additional examples of place-based policy and its implementation. The Finnish Centre of Expertise Program (CoE 1994–2013) and the Swedish Regional

Growth through Dynamic Innovation Systems Program (VINNVÄXT 2003–present) are examples of place-sensitive policies. Both programmes are based on a combination of bottom-up and top-down approaches, in which place-based local strategies meet place-sensitive national coordination. One of the guiding principles in both programmes is competition between regions, which is believed to increase collaboration locally and regionally, and boost the quality of the proposals.

Regions need to mobilise key actors for the identification of the core assets and construction of shared development strategies. Regional proposals have to include representatives from higher education institutions, businesses, and local and regional authorities (who usually coordinate the mobilisation and formulation of the proposal). Proposals are evaluated nationally, and the best are included in the programme. The main ambition was for regions to become internationally competitive in their respective fields over the life of the programme. The regional centres of expertise (Finland) or VINNVÄXT winners (Sweden) are organised somewhat differently from place to place, reflecting place-leadership and organisational capacity.

In both Sweden and Finland policy supports strategy formulation and the mobilisation of local/regional resources in order to achieve nationally set goals. The participating regions formulate a strategy reflecting their own needs. Selected regional initiatives receive modest seed funding from government, which they use to organise activities, manage networks and generate additional funding. For example, the core funding for the CoE period of 2007–11 was €40 million, while total project funding was €195 million. In Sweden, seed funding stood around €1 million per year (per initiative) for each of 10 years.

In Finland, the CoE programme was the only national-level development programme focusing on clusters, regional economic development, and innovation. From eight regions (city-regions, in practice) of the first programme period (1994–98), the second CoE programme (1999–2006) expanded to cover activities in regions that were significantly smaller and less knowledge intensive than before (14 regions and two networks). At the same time, the non-technological fields of expertise – such as cultural business, chamber music, experience industry, design and new media – were incorporated into the programme. The further expansion of the programme into new regions took place in 2003 when the number of centres implementing the CoE programme in 2003–06 totalled 22, of which 18 were regional centres and four were networked centres with operations in more than one region.[5]

The goals of the CoE programme evolved with the changing economic landscape and the meta-rationales of policy-making. The early stages of the programme were based on sectoral technology policy, but in 2011 the CoE programme was inundated by the search for practices for broad-based innovation policy. The third CoE programme period (2007–13) introduced a new operational model. It moved to stress the pooling of regional resources and competence at a national level, and for these purposes, it introduced a new concept and focus. 'Competence cluster' became the central organising concept and the key focusing device in efforts to enhance regional specialisation and boost cooperation between regions. At the same time there was a belief that competence clusters needed to be made larger in order to use more efficiently national resources scattered in different regions and enhance the international appeal of these industries by boosting their innovative activities. Moreover, it was argued that a cluster-based model might lead the attention of regional players away from competition between regions (which was common) and towards increased international competition.[6]

In Sweden from the beginning of the VINNVÄXT programme, regions were defined in functional terms, instead of following traditional administrative boundaries. Additionally, the programme adopted a broad view on innovation and explicitly tried to bypass the conventional high-tech/low-tech divide, focusing on platform strategies applicable to high-tech as well as low-tech projects. The first generation included such industries as robotics, biotechnology and food production. Later, ICT for process industries, various applications of biomedicine, and new niches for steel production, fibre optic, healthcare, industrial/environmental biotechnology, innovative textiles, geographical information systems, smart housing, and the experience industry were included in the programme.

Both programmes aimed to enhance learning at local/regional levels and to improve learning capacity among the core actors. The VINNVÄXT programme presents itself as follows:

The Vinnväxt programme – innovation in place-based policy

Politics/policy

- Provide a new policy tool for dialogue and collaboration in the form of innovative approaches.
- Put the regions 'on the map'.

Companies

- Companies connected to initiatives make better progress than others.
- Enhances distinctly cooperation with universities and research institutes.

The innovation system

- VINNVÄXT has made 'Triple Helix' common knowledge throughout Sweden.
- VINNVÄXT has strengthened the regional innovation systems and regional support structures.

Research

- VINNVÄXT initiatives attract leading researchers.
- Contribute to the development of research in universities more resources, higher quality.
- Puts research in a larger context.

Companies

- Strengthens R&D capacity as well as business and product development.
- Oldest initiatives have the strongest effect (12.13 years) on companies' development.[7]

VINNVÄXT is seen as a tool for Smart Specialisation, and the CoE programme also followed the same principles as Smart Specialisation. All in all, the programmes were, and are, essential tools in raising the strategic awareness of innovation and in building learning and innovation capacities in Sweden and Finland. The underlying ambition with such a top-down construction that explicitly encouraged bottom-up initiatives was to address system failures in a more customised way than traditional regional innovation policy. The programme was designed to promote long-term sustainable innovation support, taking into account the specific needs and available resources in respective regions. As Cai et al.[8] argue, the Centre of Expertise Programme enhanced dialogue between: (1) national and local policy actors; (2) the public sector, firms and universities across the governance levels; and (3) the public sector, firms and universities locally. It might be labelled as focused and coordinated 'multi-scalar triple helix policies' that was targeted to support clustered specialisation.[9]

In sum, the Centre of Expertise and the VINNVÄXT programmes provided a platform for collaboration between those operating at different governance levels to improve place sensitivity both nationally and regionally, while seeking to mobilise key stakeholders under a single umbrella.

4.4 PLACED-BASED INNOVATION POLICIES AND THE ROLE OF TIME FRAME AND SUPPORT BY POLITICAL LEADERS: SOUTH MORAVIA, CZECHIA

In Czechia, there is considerable variation in the way, and the extent to which, self-governing regions employ innovation policy. South Moravia is generally considered a forerunner in this field with the region starting to pioneer its own innovation policy 17 years ago. It did so in response to the shock induced by the withdrawal of a major foreign investor who settled in the regional capital (city of Brno) just four years previously. Regional stakeholders became fully aware of the vulnerabilities associated with policies focused on attracting foreign investors.

The key stakeholders took their inspiration for a new, strongly placed-based, approach from several advanced regions in Western Europe, as well as from the conceptual advances in the sphere of regional development and innovation support, especially regional innovation system theory. The main ambition from the beginning of this place-based effort was to develop a modern innovation system. This goal was to be achieved primarily via identification and engagement of key regional stakeholders and leaders, and by support for networking at both the intra- and interregional scales. It was expected this would enhance localised learning. Moreover, efforts were directed at the development of a favourable institutional framework for innovation, including the promotion of trust and an overall innovative 'atmosphere'.

In 2003, the key stakeholders (three regional universities, the regional office and the city office of Brno) jointly established The South Moravian Innovation Centre (JIC), which became the crucial driver in the formation of a modern regional innovation system. The JIC aimed to provide a set of support services targeting firms, especially start-ups and later also mature companies. It set out to develop a range of measures for start-ups and small and medium-sized enterprises (SMEs), as well as networking initiatives.

The JIC endeavoured to develop and steer the Regional Innovation Strategy while also running four business incubators. Over time, the portfolio of activities of the JIC broadened and it became subject to a regular policy-learning cycle. The working groups originally used during the elaboration of strategic documents were gradually engaged in a permanent process whereby the stakeholders (both from the public and private sectors) oversaw the implementation of approved projects, and proposed new projects and activities (Figure 4.1).

Figure 4.1 Regional innovation strategy

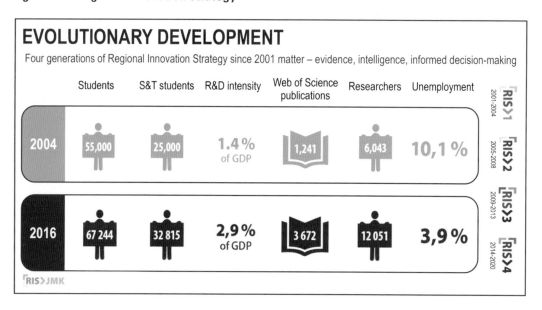

Based on an analyses of the business and research and development (R&D) institutions in the region, the following sectors with proven international competitiveness were identified within the Smart Specialisation Strategy (RIS3):

- Advanced manufacturing and engineering technologies.

- Precision instruments.

- Development of software and hardware.

- Pharmaceuticals.

- Medical care and diagnostics.

- Technologies for the aircraft industry.

The firms and R&D teams from these specialisations represent the main (but not the sole) focus of the regional innovation policy.

Looking back, two principal preconditions for this success are evident. First, the South Moravia case shows the key role of trust among the regional stakeholders. This trust took a considerable effort and time to develop. In reflecting upon the experience of South Moravia, it is clear that trust can be promoted by modest initial expectations and the acceptance of marginal gains early on. While an emphasis on result orientation is needed from the start, strict pressure to deliver rigid targets would be misleading and would hinder the learning process. It would also impede experimentation in the development of new policy.

Another challenge is the ability of key stakeholders and especially of public funders to accept failures, and as the South Moravia experience has shown, some failure is unavoidable. In this region, risk aversion amongst public funders was moderated via close collaboration between policy designers and implementing bodies, and via an effective learning/evaluation cycle enabling swift policy adjustments. Time itself is a factor, because it took approximately 10 years to build capabilities and trust among key stakeholders in South Moravia and to deliver tangible results. Consequently, such placed-based approaches do not offer quick solutions, but as the South Moravia example illustrates, the benefits occur only after a period of intensive and coordinated effort by key regional actors.

Second, the strong backing of the JIC by key stakeholders, especially by the regional government office, provided fundamental and indispensable assets upon which regional innovation policy flourished. Political support had to be developed and sustained by a careful and sensitive approach across electoral cycles – the JIC managers used every opportunity to liaise informally with the leaders of the opposition parties at the level of the region and of the city of Brno. They would explain the rationale of the JIC's activities and secure their support, while also demonstrating tangible results. Consequently, the JIC was able to sustain its position within the region even in periods of political upheaval. This 'awareness-raising policy' was crucial as the activities performed by the JIC can bear fruit only with a significant time lag (Figure 4.2).

Figure 4.2 Evolutionary development

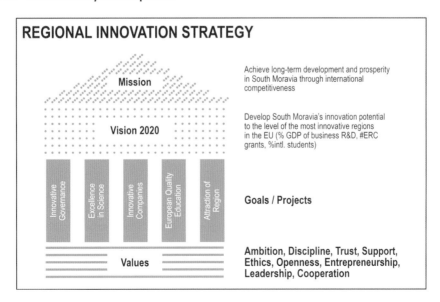

At least three broad achievements should be highlighted:

- Locally based companies expanded significantly, and this growth has been strengthened by dozens of promising start-ups and scale-ups.

- The local business sector has been enhanced by the arrival of global corporations taking advantage of the high standards of local public research. The most remarkable was the US company Honeywell, which set-up its largest R&D centre in Europe in Brno in 2003 in the premises left over by the foreign investor who left the region. Honeywell's R&D centre opened up the possibility of local companies cooperating within these knowledge networks, and this in turn has served as a role model for other corporations in the region.

- The enhanced networking and institutional capacity built within the region has enabled the effective use of European Union Structural Funds, which contributed substantially to the transformation of the region.

Over the last years, more than €700 million were invested in the construction of research centres and related infrastructure, including four centres of excellence and 11 regional centres of applied research (these centres employ over 1500 researchers).[10]

According to the latest Regional Innovation Scoreboard 2019, the South Moravia region belongs in the 'moderate+' category, and it was heading towards the status of a strong innovator. South Moravian innovation policy and its achievements inspire not only other Czech regions but also the national government.

4.5 PLACE-BASED ADAPTATION USING COLLABORATIVE GOVERNANCE: NOVA SCOTIA, CANADA

Climate change is exerting an impact on coastal regions and settlements globally. A rise in sea levels will affect all coastal settlements, and many fishing communities will also experience the consequence of global warming on the fisheries that form the central pillar of their economy. This case study is taken from the Atlantic coast of Canada and illustrates both the global reach of place-based policies and their applicability to diverse policy domains – including adaptation to climate change.

In the early 2000s, a regional adaptation collaborative (RAC) was established in Nova Scotia under the auspices of the Partnership for Canada–Caribbean Community Climate Change Adaptation (ParCA). This initiative set out to provide capacity support for vulnerable small to medium-sized coastal communities grappling with climate change and looking for better ways to improve local practice.[11] The collaborative specifically sought ways to integrate municipal or local-level responses to climate change with sector-based strategies often developed at the national level, without reference to regional variations or local needs. In implementing this initiative local authorities recognised that while several measures to ensure the future of the lobster fishery were already in place at the national or international levels, little attempt had been made to translate these arrangements to action locally.

Places with an established history of lobster fishing could potentially be disadvantaged as national regulations ensured sustainable catch limits. They could also be affected by being forced to cease harvesting and/or processing as a consequence of the loss of critical infrastructure in climate change-related events. The collaborative governance of the marine economy in Nova Scotia serves to highlight both the value of place-based policies and their capacity to operate alongside spatially blind policies for the benefit of society, the environment and the economy.

In 2009, the Canadian government established an intergovernmental and multilevel RAC programme with the aim of addressing local adaptation concerns within communities. This partnership took the form of an arrangement between provincial and municipal agencies that sought to foster partnerships for adaptation planning at the regional level and implement local-level adaptations (e.g., more appropriate infrastructure, improved planning) and participatory decision-making.

Six RAC programmes were instituted for adaptation planning and implementation across Canada. The Atlantic Climate Adaptation Solutions (ACAS) project sits within this framework and covers four provinces in the Atlantic Canadian region: Nova Scotia, New Brunswick, Newfoundland and Labrador, and Prince Edward Island. Within this plan, there is a specific focus on emergency management, coastal flood-risk mapping and best-practice guidelines for adaptation planning – including economic development.

At the same time, the Canadian government implemented policies that sought to manage fisheries to minimise the risks to both biodiversity and local economies. The lobster industry alone generates C$0.5 billion in revenues and is Nova Scotia's largest export. At the level of individual municipalities, there was a focus on (1) community planning to deal with flooding and coastal resource management; (2) developing the capacity to deal with drought and uncontrolled fires; and (3) hazards mitigation including storms and tidal events.

The RAC, as place-based policy, was able to integrate sectoral and local policies to deliver a cohesive and effective strategy for managing the impacts of climate change. It provided a mechanism for working across the federal, provincial and municipal tiers of government, while also involving the community and industry. Its achievements included:

- monitoring biophysical and ecosystem changes at the pre-harvest stage, including the implementation of ecosystem-based management;

- protecting critical industry infrastructure – including wetlands that can better manage flood risk; and

- securing local livelihoods through labour market reforms and the protection of processing plants and other assets.

Overall, the development of a place-based approach to climate adaptation resulted in the integration of sector-wide and local policies, which in turn led to better communication across a range of stakeholders, the development of innovative policy solutions, the mainstreaming of climate change policy within a broader sustainability agenda and the establishment of clear priorities for investment. Critically, the implementation of this RAC was a significant step forward in achieving a state of preparedness for a region vulnerable to climate change. The need to adapt to a changing climate has generated policy challenges that cut across the tiers of government and the public sector/private sector divide. In this instance, place-based policy seamlessly integrated at the local level the interests and responsibilities of multiple actors. It made significant advances towards ensuring the sustainability of the lobster fishery, and industry responsible for 14% of employment and a significant proportion of regional exports.

4.6 PLACE-BASED POLICY TO ADDRESS ECONOMIC DISADVANTAGE: CITY OF IIDA, NAGANO PREFECTURE, JAPAN

The city of Iida in Nagano Prefecture, Japan, is a predominantly rural region dealing with vulnerabilities similar to those confronting many rural communities around the globe. Its economy:

- offers employment that is relatively low wage;

- must accommodate and support an ageing population;

- is marked by a widely dispersed workforce, which makes it difficult to meet the needs of individual communities;

- has poor access to services for which the costs of provision are high; and

- has a sense of disempowerment and exclusion in many segments of the population.[12]

A major, and unanticipated development in Japan's economy has generated the opportunity for the city of Iida to implement place-based policies with the capacity to create new growth pathways. On 11 March 2011, the Fukushima nuclear disaster resulted in the shutdown of all nuclear power generation in Japan, which triggered a debate on the creation of a decentralised, community-led energy generation system based on renewable resources. This new system of power generation can be thought of as an example of place-based policy that meets economy-wide needs and makes use of asset-based community development to rejuvenate local economies.

One of the communities to take up the challenge of a new approach to energy generation and distribution was Iida city, an urban centre with a population of approximately 104,000 located in the southern part of Japan's Nagano Prefecture. Although administratively designated as a 'city', many smaller communities are situated in the surrounding mountain areas of the southern and central alps. More than 80% of the city's administrative area is covered by forest. The city has an ageing and declining population, and the city government has established a goal to stabilise the population at 100,000 over the long term. Recent policies have set out to identify and mobilise local assets to secure the future for current and coming generations.

Energy generation has been recognised as an economic opportunity for Iida city and its region, but the implementation of a devolved approach to power supply and distribution represents a substantial break from Japan's developmental state tradition. Beginning in the mid-1990s, the city began to develop strategies to strengthen its environmental standing and economic resilience, and in 2009, it was selected as an 'Eco Model City' by the Panel on Creating Environment Model Cities and Low Carbon Society, within the Prime Minister's Office. Iida was well suited to the challenge of generating 'green' energy, with the region receiving a significant number of hours of sunshine each year. Under the leadership of the mayor, a solar power company was established to install the nation's first solar power generation using municipal land and buildings, as well as home installations. Other initiatives soon followed, including a joint venture with the region's power distribution supplier and community-level investment in additional capacity.

Many other social enterprises followed, resulting in substantial investment in electricity generation from renewable sources. The creation of this new industry resulted in employment in the installation of capacity including small-scale hydroelectricity, but also in new plants producing photovoltaic cells and other renewable technologies. Overall, the most recent census data suggest that the establishment of this new industry based on asset-based community development slowed the rate of population loss from this rural region. Key factors in the city of Iida's success include:

- the implementation of a bottom-up approach, with local government taking advantage of national policy reform to generate new opportunities for its community;

- the capacity to work in partnership, both public–private collaborations and through the use of independent experts from outside the region;

- the implementation of an integrated strategy that brings together issues around the economy, ecology and energy; and

- the sharing of lessons learned with other communities, both within the region and more broadly.[13]

The city of Iida is a pivotal case study in that an economy-wide appetite to examine local solutions to addressing climate change, boosted by the impact of an energy crisis, has reshaped the future of this region. Along the way, it has contributed to the reshaping of power generation and energy policy nationally, and shown that a community-led approach can deliver procedural fairness and accountability with respect to opportunities to participate and the distribution of benefits.

4.7 CONCLUSIONS

This chapter has considered five case studies of place-based policy. The examples illustrate both the global ubiquity of place-based approaches and their capacity to be applied to a wide variety of challenges for public policy. The case studies also varied considerably in their scale and strategic intent: the policies implemented in the city of Iida and marine innovation in Nova Scotia were both implemented as a defensive strategy: preserving fishery resources and livelihoods in the latter instance, and the city population in the former. By contrast, the place-based polices of South Moravia, on the one hand, and Sweden and Finland, on the other, were more forward-looking, mobilising local capacities to drive innovation and economic growth. There was considerable variation also in the origin of the policies: in Japan, the city of Iida – a local government – was the primary catalyst for innovation. In Gippsland, Victoria, and South Moravia, Czechia, regional or state governments lead the process of policy experimentation, while the VINNVÄXT and CoE programmes reflected the ambitions and drivers of national governments, and their willingness to use both 'top-down' and 'bottom-up' processes to achieve their objectives.

The case studies present the rich variety that is place-based policy but also several common threads. One such thread is the importance of working across governments and in association with the broader community. In South Moravia, Gippsland, as well as in Finland and Sweden, collaboration across the tiers of government and the spectrum of organisations was a central element of the policy design, while in Japan and Sweden the investment decisions of civil society organisations and the private sector were critical to achieving programme objectives. In all instances polices were developed and implemented across a considerable time frame with a 10-year horizon embedded in the policy design of the VINNVÄXT programme and evident in the period to success in South Moravia. Finally, we can observe that understanding what success looks like – a shift to sustainable energy and population levels in Japan; globally competitive industries in Finland and Sweden; ongoing employment for affected workers in the Latrobe Valley – were all critical for defining each place-based policy.

At a broader level, the case studies highlight the fact that place-based policies can be successful under a wide range of circumstances, with different systems of government, variable resourcing, diverse aims and objectives, and diverse cultural context and economic systems. From the case studies we can conclude *that it is the process of implementation that determines whether a place-based policy will achieve its goals. Place-based policies require more than just the policy-setting and programme-design capacities: the nature, duration and collaborative approach used to bring them to life are critical.*

REFERENCES

1   Latrobe Valley Authority (2019) *Transitioning to a Strong Future, Latrobe Valley Community Report, November 2016– November 2019*. Melbourne: Victoria State Government, p. 2.

2   Mike Timpano, Director Education and Innovation, Latrobe Valley Authority, and Karen Cain, CEO, Latrobe Valley Authority, personal communications with Fiona McKenzie, 20 September 2019.

3   Personal communications with both Timpano and Cain, see Reference 2.

4   Latrobe Valley Authority (2019), see Reference 1.

5   Wallin J and Laxell P (2013) *Alueet globaaleissa ekosysteemeissä Osaamiskeskusohjelman loppuarviointi. Työ- ja elinkeinoministeriön julkaisuja*. Innovaatio 19/2013. Helsinki: Työ- ja elinkeinoministeriö.

6   Sotarauta M (2012) Policy learning and the 'cluster flavoured innovation policy' in Finland. *Environment and Planning C: Government and Policy*, 30(5): 780–795.

7   *Vinnväxt, A Program Renewing and Moving Sweden ahead* (2016). Vinnova Information VI 2016:8. Stockholm: Vinnova.

8   Cai Y, Normann R, Pinheiro R and Sotarauta M (2018) Economic specialization and diversification at the country and regional level: Introducing a conceptual framework to study innovation policy logics. *European Planning Studies*, 26(12): 2407–2426.

9   Sotarauta M and Suvinen N (2018) Institutional agency and path creation: Institutional path from industrial to knowledge city. In A Saksen, R Martin and M Trippl (eds.), *New Avenues for Regional Innovation Systems – Theoretical Advances, Empirical Cases and Policy Lessons*, pp. 85–104. New York: Springer.

10 Blažek J, Květoň V, Uhlíř D, and Marek D (2019) South Moravia: From a quick fix by foreign investments towards a bottom-up policy learning? In K Koschatsky and T Stahlecker (eds.), *Innovation-Based Regional Change in Europe: Chances, Risks and Policy Implications*, pp. 93–118. Stuttgart: Fraunhofer.

11 Khan A, Charles A and Armitage D (2018) Place-based or sector-based adaptation? A case study of municipal and fishery policy integration. *Climate Policy*, 18(1): 14–23.

12 Feldhoff T (2016) Asset-based community development in the energy sector: Energy and regional policy lessons for community power in Japan. *International Planning Studies*, 21(3): 261–77.

13 Feldhoff (2016), see Reference 12.

5. CONCLUSIONS: QUESTIONS ANSWERED, ISSUES REMAINING

This Policy Expo set out to show how place-based policy makes a positive contribution to the productivity and well-being of national, regional and local economies. Using published work, as well as policy experience globally, it set out to identify the determinants of success in the development and implementation of place-based policies, while also seeking to understand when, how and why such approaches were developed and deployed. In undertaking this analysis, we acknowledged that, over the past decade, increased attention has been paid to place-based policy-making. This focus has been evident throughout Europe, the North Americas and Australia, but also in developing economies. Place-based policies have been applied to an array of policy domains, including the provision of social services, responses to entrenched social dysfunction and in the formation of better industry policy.[1]

This Policy Expo set out to provide answers to the following questions:

1. How can governments and communities best deliver place-based policy?
2. What are the barriers to, and enablers of, the successful implementation of place-based policies?
3. What is the role of city or regional leadership in place-based policy? And what is the relationship with systems of governance?
4. Can we identify instances of the successful implementation of place-based policies?
5. What are the key lessons for policy-makers, the academic community and major institutions seeking to enable place-based policy?
6. How can we build a community of practice around placed-based policy in order to enable better social, economic and environmental outcomes?

Each question will be addressed in turn, and the overarching findings of the Expo will be discussed.

5.1 HOW CAN GOVERNMENTS AND COMMUNITIES BEST DELIVER PLACE-BASED POLICY?

The overwhelming finding from this research is that governments and communities can best deliver place-based policy through a collaborative approach – one that is: sensitive to the needs of each locality; recognizes, and makes use of, the emotional attachment individuals have the places in which they live; and allows for the sharing of decision-making power.

Unlike spatially blind policies, the success of place-based policies is largely determined by how well they are implemented, rather than designed, and the willingness of all stakeholders to breathe life into the ambitions of the policy on an ongoing basis. Governments seeking to deliver place-based policy need to pay attention to the 10 key determinants of success in place-based policy discussed in chapter 3, section 4 (Box 5.1).

We would also argue that there are two critical preconditions for success in place-based policy. First, good governance arrangements are essential if place-based policies and programmes are to achieve their goals. This means that the arrangements that provide oversight of such initiatives must include an appropriate mix of stakeholders, including those representative of disadvantaged groups, as well as those with the power to bring about change through the organizations they lead or work within, as well as the resources

https://doi.org/10.1080/2578711X.2020.1783901

> **Box 5.1   Ten key determinants of success in place-based policy:**
>
> 1. Develop an explicit focus on place and work to make use of the full set of opportunities and resources in that locality.
> 2. Foster an engagement with local institutions to achieve the mission of each place-based policy.
> 3. Focus on governance, accepting the need to create robust, sustainable and transparent processes, and acknowledging the key role of erudite and charismatic leaders.
> 4. Emphasize value creation and the local capture of value in order to generate opportunities in the short, medium and long terms.
> 5. Acknowledge the need to consider the performance of places over a long time frame.
> 6. Prioritize the assistance to those individuals and groups for whom adjustment processes are most challenging.
> 7. Accept that there is an emotional dimension to questions of place and the future of places which may be especially evident in periods of rapid change – such as disruption to local industries – but is present in all circumstances.
> 8. Incorporate outcome and output measures – qualitative and quantitative – early in the implementation of place-based initiatives in order to drive achievement.
> 9. Avoid faltering expectations and a cycle of disillusionment by having demonstrable, significant achievements built into the programme design. These can be short term, long term or developmental and they need to be communicated to all stakeholders, including the wider community.
> 10. Embrace the explicit focus on the goals and aspirations of that specific place-based policy from inception, and these need to be agreed to by all stakeholders.

they contribute to this shared objective. Good governance calls for well-understood aims, but also transparent and robust processes around information-sharing and decision-making.

Second, we contend that the ability of place-based policies to achieve their objectives is not solely a function of how well they address issues of governance; they also need to connect, and engage, with the leadership in these places. Acknowledging the importance of local leaders and their communities is not an easy or simple challenge for governments and their policy-makers because it calls for the acceptance of the limits to governmental power, a sharing of resources and decision-making, and the willingness to work toward societal goods that are beyond the immediate electoral cycle.

5.2   WHAT ARE THE BARRIERS TO, AND ENABLERS OF, THE SUCCESSFUL IMPLEMENTATION OF PLACE-BASED POLICIES?

There are numerous barriers to the successful implementation of place-based policies, but perhaps the most significant challenge is the failure of some to acknowledge that *every place matters* – that every community, no matter how small or poor, is important because it represents someone's home, a source of livelihoods, a sense of place and belonging to those who reside there, and an opportunity for children and adults alike to grow and develop.

The material presented throughout this Expo, and especially the case studies, emphasizes that place-based policies can achieve their goals and deliver substantial benefits for the target communities and at-risk individuals within them. Some places may be primed for success, and these might include localities with an already strong sense of regional identity, strong bridging and bonding social capital, places with a history of innovation and adapting to change, and a skilled and well-educated population able to adapt to new opportunities. The quality of leadership and the quality of government also plays a determining role, as does the strength of civil society organizations.

5.3 WHAT IS THE ROLE OF CITY OR REGIONAL LEADERSHIP IN PLACE-BASED POLICY, AND WHAT IS THE RELATIONSHIP WITH SYSTEMS OF GOVERNANCE?

City or regional leadership is an essential component of the success of place-based policies. It is through local leaders that government programmes achieve the recognition and 'buy in' of the local community, while at the same time local leaders assist the policy achieve its objectives by mobilizing resources from across the community. This leadership can be part of the formal system of governance, through the incorporation of mayors or other local political leaders into the policy process, or it could be outside government entirely, relying on place leaders who draw their influence from their standing in the community and their ability to imagine and communicate a better future.

Critically, the involvement of leaders must include a sharing of power; consultation is insufficient genuine decision-making power needs to be negotiated and enacted.

5.4 CAN WE IDENTIFY INSTANCES OF THE SUCCESSFUL IMPLEMENTATION OF PLACE-BASED POLICIES?

There are many instances of the successful implementation of place-based policies, and examples are provided in this book:

- In South Moravia, the implementation of a place-based programme over 10 years resulted in the region's capacity to innovate rising considerably.

- In Finland and Sweden, national-level programmes implemented at the level of places or regions enhanced productive capacity and fuelled the rise of new industries.

- In Nova Scotia, a place-based approach resulted in the better governance of marine resources.

- In Japan similar policy frameworks delivered both economic growth and sustainable energy to a relatively remote part of that island nation.

Additional searching, of course, would result in further instances of success in place-based policy. Critically, the successes are many, but so too are the perceived failures, and think tanks, academic researchers and government bodies are right to call out examples of waste or the misallocation of resources. However, often such apparent failures reflect deficiencies introduced at their inception: the failure to address questions of governance adequately, no or unrealistic goals and objectives, and exclusion of the community and its leaders. These could be overcome if there was a more robust evidence base available to policy-makers.

5.5 WHAT ARE THE KEY LESSONS FOR POLICY-MAKERS, THE ACADEMIC COMMUNITY AND MAJOR INSTITUTIONS SEEKING TO ENABLE PLACE-BASED POLICY?

The most important lesson to come from this research is that success is possible. Indeed, it is not only possible but also achievable in most policy domains, under a variety of governmental structures – federations, unitary systems and others – and at a variety of scales. Success, however, calls for a commitment to:

- understand good practice in place-based policy;

- commit to implementing these policies over an extended period; and

- enact those commitments through strong governance arrangements, a commitment to the dissemination of outcomes and the ongoing evaluation of priorities.

The research also has key lessons for the academic community. There is a pressing need for both better instruments for the measurement of the outcomes of place-based policies and a more engaged, outward-looking, discussion with broader society about the benefits these initiatives deliver across the community. There is a need for more case studies, and more discussion of case studies, because as Flyvbjerg[2] observed, case studies provide both an important analytical device and a readily accessible tool with which to communicate to a broader audience.

5.6 HOW CAN WE BUILD A COMMUNITY OF PRACTICE AROUND PLACE-BASED POLICY IN ORDER TO ENABLE BETTER SOCIAL, ECONOMIC AND ENVIRONMENTAL OUTCOMES?

There is a pressing need for a community of practice around place-based policy, and this community needs better access to information, an opportunity to reach out to others through a formal network that spans nations and sectors, and through the sharing of experiences.

In commissioning this Policy Expo, the Regional Studies Association has taken a first step towards the creation of this community of practice, but it would be inappropriate to suggest a responsibility for implementation lies with it alone. Many other organizations have a strong investment in, or commitment to, the success of place-based policy and potential participants, including: the Organisation for Economic Co-operation and Development (OECD); the European Union and its constituent Directorate Generals; LD Net and its operations across Europe; practitioner organizations such as Economic Development Australia; and national governments. There is a need for knowledge that has been codified in publications, but also opportunities to share experiences at conferences and webinars.

This community of practice would potentially lead to better outcomes for affected communities, while simultaneously removing the 'conceptual confusion' decried by some researchers. It would create the opportunity for better research that is more impactful, and which leads to further conceptual advances.

5.7 FINAL OBSERVATIONS

The discussion of place-based policy inevitably challenges our understanding of both 'place' and 'policy'. It forces us to reconsider what is a place, as some place-based policies find expression at a very small scale, while others are large programmes enacted over broad regions. As discussed in this book, there is an emotional element to 'place' and it is not sufficient to think of places and the actions needed to support them without taking account of this subjective element.

Place-based policy, however, presents an even greater challenge when we think of the 'policy' component. In an era when government expenditures and outlays are increasingly contested, and when nation-states increasingly find themselves simultaneously challenged by global economic and political processes, as well as local discontent, place-based policy challenges the 'business as usual'. It calls for governments to behave in ways they find difficult: the sharing of power, the planning and working towards difficult-to-achieve long-term goals, and the surrender of freedom to act as they would choose in future because of long-term commitments.

There can be no denying that there are significant impediments to the implementation of successful place-based policies, but for many parts of the contemporary global economy there is no alternative. As Rodríguez-Pose[3] has observed, spatially blind policies have left too many places behind, resulting in political and economic uncertainty. The only solution is the implementation of place-based policies that can help every region, city, industry and community reach its potential.

REFERENCES

1. Bailey D, Pitelis C and Tomlinson P (2018) A place-based developmental regional industrial strategy for sustainable capture and co-created value. *Cambridge Journal of Economics*, 42(6): 1521–1542.
2. Flyvberg B (2006) Five misunderstandings about case study research. *Qualitative Inquiry*, 12(2): 219–245.
3. Rodríguez-Pose A. (2018) The revenge of the places that don't matter (and what to do about it). *Cambridge Journal of Regions, Economy and Society*, 11(1): 189–209.

GLOSSARY

Endogenous growth. Growth that arises in a city or region as a result of its natural growth potential and assets rather than as a consequence of significant change – new investment or labour force change – driven by external forces.

Entrepreneurial-discovery process. Describes a key component of Smart Specialisation Strategies. The engagement of entrepreneurs in a city or region in identifying new technologies that can fuel the further growth of existing industries.

Functional areas. Areas that function as a single labour market or economic unit. Commonly functional areas spill beyond the formal boundaries of cities or regions.

Governance. Describes the ways in which government seeks to draw on the resources and abilities of external individuals and agencies to achieve its goals. Governance arrangements implicitly involve the sharing of decision-making power.

Human capital. The skills, capacities and talents of the workforce. Human capital is seen to rise as educational attainment and training increases.

Just Transition. A process of structural change within an industry where workers are seen to be treated 'justly' as the sector contracts or closes completely.

Path dependency. Describes how the possibilities for future economic growth are shaped by history, including prior industries, infrastructure investments and labour force attributes.

Place-based policy. Policies that seek to encourage the development of a locality – socially, economically, culturally or environmentally – through actions tailored to the specific requirements of that place.

Place-neutral policy. Policies that neither help nor hinder the development of cities and regions being provided uniformly across the landscape.

https://doi.org/10.1080/2578711X.2020.1783903

Smart Specialisation. An economic strategy that seeks to encourage the growth of regions by introducing new technologies that are potentially beneficial to the existing industry base, thereby driving productivity growth, a stronger market presence and long-term sustainability.

Spatially blind policy. Policies that do not explicitly pay attention to their impacts on different parts of the territory of a nation or other territory, instead placing their priorities elsewhere, including accelerating national income. The implementation of such policies may operate to the benefit of some localities and to the disadvantage of others.

Value creation. Summarises the way in which economic activity creates wealth for businesses, individuals, and cities and regions.